THE BRITISH ARMY IN THE AMERICAN REVOLUTION

Alan Kemp

ALMARK PUBLISHING CO LTD, LONDON

© Almark Publishing Co Ltd, 1973
Text and artwork © Alan Kemp

All rights reserved. No part of this publication may be reproduced, stored in a retrieval system, or transmitted by any means, electronic, mechanical, or by photo copying without prior permission from the publishers.

First Published—September 1973

ISBN 0 85524 143 8 (hard cover edition)
ISBN 0 85524 144 6 (paper covered edition)

Printed in Great Britain by
Staples Printers Limited at The Priory Press, St Albans
Hertfordshire for the publishers, Almark Publishing Co Ltd
270 Burlington Road, New Malden,
Surrey KT3 4NL, England

Introduction

AT the outbreak of the American Revolution there were just over 11,500 British troops in North America. By mid-1776 the number had increased to 27,000 men, including 2,000 Marines.

The British Government had experienced great difficulty in recruiting sufficient men to bring the army up to its required strength. Conditions in the army were not conducive to easy recruitment and it was said that many of the social class from which the rank and file were drawn supported the struggle for liberty then being waged by the American patriots and were loathe to take up arms against them. It must be added, however, that difficulty in recruiting had been experienced since the beginning of the 18th century.

Whatever the reasons, the necessary numbers of men were not forthcoming, despite the lures of a £3 bounty for enlistment in a Line regiment or the £6 offered to recruits in the Guards. The usual practice of not recruiting Roman Catholics was relaxed and at least three regiments were made up almost solely from occupants of the country's overcrowded prisons.

Notwithstanding these efforts at raising an army the Crown was obliged to call on the services of mercenaries from various German states to assist in the struggle to retain the American colonies.

The record of the British Army in America stands up well to scrutiny. After the harrowing experience of some forty days of harsh privations on board a rotting transport a soldier could expect to campaign under officers who were often less than competent and to suffer neglect as a result of the misappropriation of funds by Government ministers at home, lining their own pockets from the war budget.

The army in America was guilty of none of the excesses which marked its passage in later wars, such as the Peninsular campaign. Despite being goaded by the brutal methods of partisan warfare waged by savage patriots the soldiers showed a great measure of restraint.

The American Revolution was a war with few opportunities for the set-piece battles previously experienced by the British Army in 18th-century Europe. From the American standpoint it was generally in their interest to avoid pitched battles whenever possible. Their citizen army was no match for the disciplined volleys and fearsome bayonet charges of professional soldiers. Although not always possible, the patriots did try to avoid open clashes, relying more on hit and run tactics and with the emphasis on concealed sharpshooters.

However, it did not take long for the British soldier to adapt himself to these tactics. Within a few months, under the instruction of Loyalist Rangers and Indians, the redcoats, particularly the men of the Light companies, were giving a good account of themselves in the guerilla methods of forest warfare.

This irregular manner of waging war coupled with difficulties of supply made it necessary for the British soldier to adapt his clothing and equipment. Transports were often captured or lost on the long Atlantic crossing and utility costume would have been much in evidence after a short period of wilderness campaigning.

In this book I have tried to deal with both how the British soldier should have appeared during the Revolution following the specifications of the Official Warrant, and how he did appear according to narratives and graphic material from contemporary sources.

CONTENTS

Section	Page
Introduction	*3*
1: Organization and Tactics	*7*
2: Infantry Uniforms	*12*
3: Artillery Uniforms	*43*
4: Cavalry Uniforms	*52*
5: Colours	*58*
Appendix A: Notes on each Regiment in America	*61*
Appendix B: Contemporary notes on Military Life	*68*
Appendix C: Special Badges	*70*
Bibliography	*72*

FRONT COVER: Battalion company man of the 16th Foot in marching order.

1: Organization and Tactics

IN recruiting for the British Army of the 18th century the authorities were not particular as to the type of man required to fill the ranks of His Majesty's regiments.

The prospects of the common soldier were anything but attractive and the numbers of recruits were maintained by every possible means. A large proportion were 'enlisted' by the press-gangs and kidnapping parties, while those who did volunteer were often criminals or men who faced unemployment and near-starvation in civilian life. Glib-tongued recruiting sergeants frequently plied gullible country lads with liquor and persuaded them to take the King's shilling whilst under the influence of this. An extract from a statute of the period gives an impression of the type of character destined to fill the ranks of the constantly under-strength battalions. 'Any sturdy beggar, any fortune teller, any idle, unknown or suspected fellow in a parish that cannot give an account of himself, he shall be taken before anyone else. . . .' It continues, '. . . any one who has been in gaol or before a justice of the peace shall be captured . . .', and further, 'anyone known as an incorrigible rogue, even if his wife and children come on the parish, because the parish will be glad to get rid of him'.

Once in the army the recruit could resign himself to a life of iron discipline under the threat of the lash. The pay for an infantry private was less than one shilling per day before off-takes for clothing, etc, and a soldier's waking hours were occupied by guard duties, cleaning and repairing equipment, and four hours every day spent drilling. What little time and money a soldier had to himself were usually spent in the pursuits of gambling and strong drink. The mid-18th century was an age notorious for over-indulgence in alcohol by all sections of the community and it was more than likely that a private soldier stumbling half-drunk on to the parade ground would be drilled by officers and NCOs in the same condition.

This then, was the calibre of the rank and file of the British Army. Despite their environment most of these misfits were destined to become excellent soldiers and acquit themselves well in a war on a continent as alien to them as the surface of the moon.

OFFICERS

In an age when the class system prevailed the officer corps of the British Army in the 1770s left much to be desired. Commissions were obtained by purchase which meant that families with sufficient wealth were able to buy responsible positions in the army for sons who were often little more than children. These 'ensigns' (or cornets in the cavalry) would carry the regimental colours until such time as a vacant lieutenancy became available and could be purchased for them.

Apart from the Artillery, there were no training schools for new officers and a subaltern would take the field with no more experience than the advice of those about him to whom he was willing to listen.

Securing a commission from the ranks was almost impossible. If an able soldier did manage to achieve this he could often find himself stranded as a lieutenant or a captain for the remainder of his career, not having the necessary funds with which to purchase a promotion. The obvious result of this system was an army with a high proportion of either inexperienced adolescents or old men as junior officers. Many commanders, including the Duke of Cumberland, realized the weaknesses of the British officer system and tried to correct it, attempting to establish methods of promoting able young officers to positions of command without regard to their financial status. They had little success, however, and the purchase system remained for another century.

A large proportion of senior commands went to those officers holding commissions in the Guards. The Brigade of Guards, being the élite of the army, attracted those men of higher birth who were financially equipped for advancement and consequently had more opportunities for promotion. A captain in the Guards was classed as being on a par with a lieutenant-colonel of a Line regiment. One out of every three regiments had a commanding officer who had served in the Guards and chances of promotion for a Line officer were slight if he was competing for a vacancy with an officer of the Guards.

There was no organized mess and officers amused themselves by drinking, gambling and quarrelling, usually at the expense of their military duties. They had little contact with their men and frequently neglected their martial careers for some other commitment, eg Burgoyne leaving America during the first winter of the war to take up his seat in the House of Commons.

The majority of senior British commanders in the American War had received their military education on the battlefields of Europe. They were hard put to it to adapt the formal tactics and strategy of past campaigns to a conflict in the wilderness of the New World. It was a popular opinion amongst interested parties of the Crown that a commander need not be too brilliant to serve in 'an American War'. It was an opinion which was to shift by 1783.

MEDICAL SERVICES

Scant attention was paid to injured men and few soldiers had much chance of survival from a severe wound or a serious infection. It is recorded that after Bunker Hill many officers died of their wounds. It follows that the plight of an enlisted man would be infinitely worse.

Surgeons were constantly overworked and had little hope of coping with the demands of a regiment's casualties. These surgeons had little social standing. They were mostly Scotsmen paid about four shillings per day, who, together with their surgeon's mates, attempted to provide succour under extremely difficult conditions and equipped with pathetically inadequate medical supplies.

The surgeon had to supply his own surgical tools, but in action these were not always to hand and he was often obliged to use whatever crude implements were available. Supplies of bandages, ointments, splints, etc were always short and the frequent use of the same sponge, coupled with an absence of antiseptics, caused many wounds to become infected. Anaesthetics were also unknown. A wounded man under the surgeon's knife faced his ordeal biting on a bullet and, if he was lucky semi-drugged by a draught of raw spirits.

ORGANIZATION OF A REGIMENT

An infantry regiment was made up of about 450 men plus another 20 or so who were known as 'contingent' and 'warrant' men. Contingent men were usually non-combatants who served to repair arms and equipment, while warrant men did not even exist but were listed as being on the regimental strength for the purpose of drawing their pay to help balance the battalion's finances, eg officers' widows fund, clothing losses, etc. The body of a regiment was made up of eight battalion or centre companies. Soldiers of these companies were known as 'hat-men' because their head-dress was the cocked hat. The centre companies were flanked on the right by a Grenadier company, wearing tall bearskin caps, and on the left by a Light company wearing small leather helmets. These two 'flank companies' were considered to be the élite of the regiment, the Grenadiers being selected from the tallest, best-looking men, while the Light company men were drawn from the smaller, sharp-witted, agile soldiers in the regiment.

During the American War both the Light companies and the Grenadier companies of the British regiments were banded together in battalion strength and served as independent bodies.

The remainder of the British Army in America was made up of two Light Dragoon regiments (16th and 17th), nine companies of the Royal Artillery and a number of Marines who fought as infantry. These are dealt with under their respective sections.

TACTICS

The principal arm on the battlefields of the 18th century was infantry, and most battle formations were based upon its use. On the march, the army would travel in column, that is, two or more lines of men. Upon reaching the battle area the soldiers would deploy into 'lines of battle' consisting of two or three ranks facing the front and having a line of reserves standing some six feet behind the rear rank. These reserves would fill the gaps caused by casualties.

On the offensive, these lines would advance with fixed bayonets to beat of drum towards the enemy, all the while being kept in formation by the halberds of the sergeants reaching out to correct the dressing of the ranks. Once within range the lines would fire a volley and carry home the charge with the bayonet.

On the defensive side, the troops would, in a textbook engagement, also be dressed in lines of battle. They would wait until the advancing lines were some 50 yards away then discharge their own volley (after having loaded in sequence to words of command). The defenders would then attempt to reload for a second and perhaps a third volley before the attacking force was upon them and hand-to-hand fighting ensued.

Accuracy of fire in aiming at individual targets was not considered. The secret of infantry attack and defence was a steady rate of fire, keeping up such a concentrated hail of shot that the enemy broke and fled. This is where the long hours of repetitive drill on the parade ground paid dividends. The British soldier was able, through this discipline, to stand amongst the carnage and load and fire at a rate of something like four shots a minute without even thinking about the firing sequence.

The commands for loading and firing were as follows:

Handle cartridge! The cartridge was drawn from the pouch in the right hand. Held between forefinger and thumb, it was brought to the mouth and the top bitten off.

Prime!	A little of the powder was shaken into the priming pan which was afterwards closed with the last three fingers. The small of the butt was then held with the same three fingers.
Load!	With the body facing slightly to the left and the right foot pointing to the front, the musket held almost vertically was brought to the left side. The butt was about two inches from the ground with the weapon sloped to the front and the muzzle steadied by the right hand. The rest of the powder was poured from the cartridge into the barrel and the wadding and ball placed in after it. The top of the ramrod, under the muzzle was then held between the forefinger and thumb of the right hand.

Make Ready   Present - Give Fire

Draw Ramrods! The ramrod was pulled half out, then held backhanded at its centre. It was then fully drawn and, with the arm extended, turned and placed one inch into the barrel.

Ram down cartridge! The ramrod was pushed into the barrel, still held in the centre, until the hand touched the muzzle. The forefinger and thumb slid to the end of the ramrod and the cartridge was pushed to the bottom of the barrel with a few quick strokes.

Return Ramrods! The ramrod was withdrawn and returned to its channel beneath the barrel, being pushed home smartly.

When the first command of 'Handle cartridge' was given, the musket was at half-cock and held at what was known as the primary position. This position varied according to which rank a man was in. In the front rank it was at the height of the waistband of the breeches (these men knelt on the right knee to fire their volley); in the centre rank it was in the middle of the stomach; in the rear rank it was close to the chest (this rank moved one pace to the right to clear the centre rank while firing a volley).

Once the loading procedure was complete the firing orders were given. The commands were:

Make ready! The musket was brought vertically up the body as the right hand sought the trigger and lock.

Present! The musket was brought, butt to shoulder and pointed at the target.

Give Fire! The musket was discharged.

2: Infantry Uniforms

BATTALION COMPANIES

AS stated previously the battalion companies made up the bulk of a Line regiment.

At the commencement of the American Revolution in 1775 the infantry of the British Army were wearing uniforms of the patterns specified in the Clothing Warrant of 1768.

The standard headgear of Battalion companies was the cocked hat. This was made of black felt with a round crown and a large brim. By 1775 the hat had just about lost the three-cornered look and was now worn with the front raised higher, almost giving the appearance of a bicorne. An order of 1771 had ruled that hats were to adopt a uniform style of cock but variations of style were much in evidence throughout the army. The hats were bound around the edge with white tape about one inch in depth and had a black cockade and loop held with a small regimental button. The tassels which ended the cord around the crown were sometimes worn hanging above the shoulders. Two pieces of tape were often sewn to the lining of the hat and fastened under the club of the hair to prevent the hat falling off or being dislodged from the set position. In the rigours of the American War it appears that the hat was sometimes worn uncocked or with one side only turned up. The practice also developed of attaching feathers or fur animal tails to the cockade. Old coats were cut up to make red forage caps. These were lined with canvas and had in front a small upright peak in the facing colour and a back flap which could be turned down to protect the neck.

The regimental coat was of red cloth lined white and reached to just above the knee. It had a fall down collar, round cuffs and lapels to the waist all in the facing colour of the regiment. The collar bore two buttons, the cuffs four each and the lapels ten each side (although variations of this number are known). The buttons were made of pewter and carried the number of the regiment and sometimes a special design.

The buttonholes were bound with lace of a regimental pattern and the skirts of the coat were held back either by a button on a strip of this lace or with a decorative metal clasp. Regiments with buff-coloured facings had their coats lined with buff linen and also wore buff waistcoats, breeches and leather equipment in place of white. The coat also had two horizontal pockets with four buttons on each and buttonholes laced with regimental lace. These pockets were purely decorative and were stitched down, the actual pockets being sewn in the lining of the coat. There were also two loops of regimental lace on each side of the centre vent at the back of the coat. According to pictorial evidence from about 1770 a shoulder strap of red cloth on the left shoulder held in place the belt holding the cartridge pouch (sometimes two shoulder straps are shown in these contemporary illustrations). To save coats from excessive wear they were sometimes worn inside out for heavy duties or on a sea voyage. It may have been the practice to shorten the coat for convenience

TYPES OF REGIMENTAL BUTTONS.
a. 17th Foot. Officers. Silver.
b. 17th Foot. Other ranks. Pewter.
c. 14th Foot. Other ranks. Pewter.
d. 18th Foot. (Royal Irish). Other ranks. Pewter.
e. 28th Foot. Officers. Silver.
f. 49th Foot. Officers in silver, men pewter (found in America).
g. 2nd Foot Guards. Pewter (found in America).
h. 3rd Foot Guards. Pewter (found in America).
i. 15th Foot. Other ranks. Pewter.
j. 29th Foot. Officers in silver, men pewter.
k. 4th Foot. Officers. Silver (found in America).
l. 10th Foot. Other ranks. Pewter (found in New York).
m. 21st Foot. Officers. Gilt.   n. 21st Foot. Other ranks. Pewter.

in the manner of the Light companies. A contemporary illustration shows men of the 40th Foot with jackets of only waist length. No pockets are shown which could indicate that the coats had been cut off above these. The absence of shoulder wings suggests that these are battalion men rather than light infantry.

Apart from those regiments with buff facings, smallclothes (waistcoat and breeches) for battalion companies were white. The single-breasted waistcoat had two small pockets and small metal buttons; 'Waistcoats for front and rear rank of Grenadiers to have twelve buttons, centre rank to have eleven. Front and rear ranks of battalion companies to have eleven buttons, centre rank to have ten.' White linen shirts were worn with black leather stocks (for full dress the stocks were black velvet trimmed with red). The breeches were buckled and buttoned on the outside of the leg just below the knee. Black gaiters reaching to just above the knee were worn by all ranks. They were buttoned down the outside of the leg, fastened under the foot and held below the knee by black garters with buckles. Sometimes that part of the gaiter which covered the knee was reinforced with leather and cut away at the back to facilitate easier movement. White linen tops under the gaiters prevented the breeches from becoming soiled. As an alternative to these high gaiters, black linen spatterdashes were worn by many troops. These reached to the swell of the calf and had the tops cut to an angle coming to a point at the back of the leg. These too were buttoned down the outside of the leg and fastened under the foot. They were worn with grey or white stockings and were preferable to the high gaiters in hot weather. A third type of legwear for the rank and file was the overall. These were combined trousers and gaiters made of canvas or linen (brown cloth for winter campaigning, white coarse duck for summer). They were fastened under the foot and buttoned half-way up the calf. All types of legwear were worn with black shoes with metal buckles.

The equipment carried consisted of a black leather cartridge pouch sometimes bearing a metal or painted badge. It was suspended over the right hip on a $2\frac{3}{4}$ inch wide buff or white shoulder belt. The bayonet in a black leather scabbard with metal fittings, hung on the left side from a 2-inch wide buff or white waistbelt. This belt was sometimes worn as a second shoulder belt over the right shoulder. This method of wearing was not made official until 1782 but had already been worn in America for some time. The shoulder belts were sometimes secured together on the chest by a metal plate bearing the regiment's number or badge. Also on the left hip, slung from the right shoulder were a grey canvas or heavy linen haversack (not worn in peace-time) and a

INFANTRY EQUIPMENT (*items not drawn to scale*).
a. Knapsack of white goatskin.
b. & c. Canteens in metal and wood.
d. Cartridge Pouch. This is a Grenadier's model with match-case attached. Notice the pricker and brush above the buckle for clearing a fouled touch-hole.
e. Bayonet in scabbard.

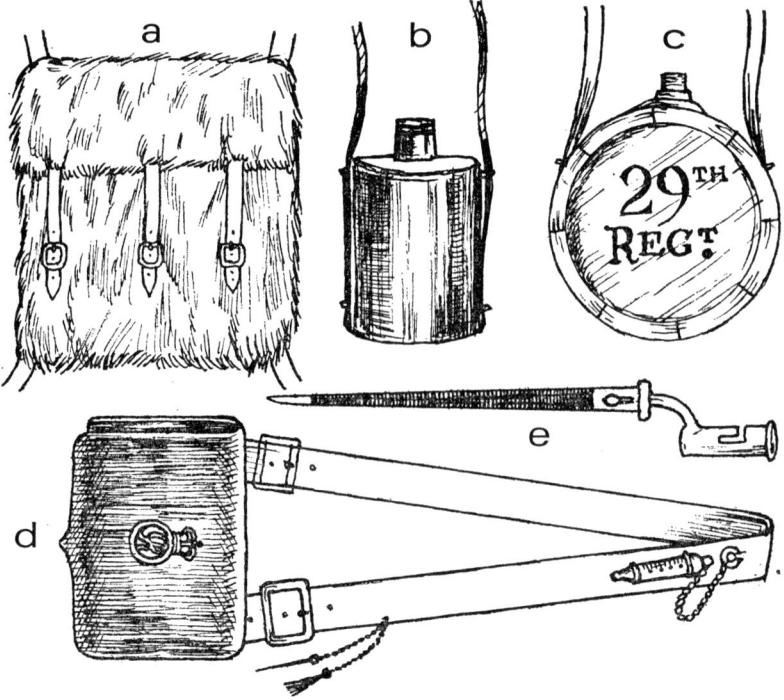

EXAMPLES OF BELT PLATES.
a. 38th Foot (found in America).
b. 37th Foot (found at Staten Island).
c. 20th Foot. Officer. (Gilt with design mounted in silver.)
d. 16th Foot. Officer. (Silver.)
e. 17th Foot. Officer (found in New York. Silver).
f. 28th Foot. Officer (found in New York. Solid Silver).
g. 2nd Foot Guards (Coldstream). Negative shapes are cut-out (found at Fort Tryon, New York City).
h. Royal Fusiliers (7th Foot) found in New York. Gun Metal.

canteen of either metal or wood. A rectangular knapsack of white goatskin was carried on the back held by buff or white shoulder straps which were linked by a securing strap across the chest. Knapsacks were often made of grey canvas. These were probably worn to preserve the goatskin one.

The soldiers' firearm was a musket of the Short Land Service (new pattern), more familiarly known as the 'Brown Bess'. This flintlock weapon had a calibre of ·75 and weighed approximately 10 pounds. It was to remain, with variations, the main arm of British infantry for over 100 years.

At this time there was no general issue of overcoats or greatcoats. Only men on guard duty in cold or inclement weather wore these. In America, however, the whole of the army with Burgoyne in the winter of 1776–77 were issued with a special overcoat. It was made of white wool with a white melton hood, and was decorated with blue braid and tied down the front to the waist with blue ribbons or rosettes. Caps with brown fur around the base and a fur tail were worn with these coats. Variations of these red caps included some made wholly of fur and others like pointed hoods. Leggings of thick blue cloth were also worn by some troops during winter. The soldiers were taught the use of snowshoes and 'creepers' (something like a climber's crampon with small spikes which fitted under the foot to prevent slipping on ice). The usual belts and equipment were worn over the wool coat which was known as a 'capote'.

GRENADIER COMPANIES

Grenadiers were usually recruited from the tallest, best-looking men in a regiment. They were also expected to be the bravest and to give inspiration to the rest of the men. For the duration of the American War grenadier companies were detached from their regiments and banded together to serve as independent battalions.

The coats of the grenadiers had additions to those of the men of the centre companies. According to the Clothing Warrant of 1768 they were to have 'round wings of red cloth on the point of the shoulder, with six loops of the same sort of lace as on the buttonholes and a border around the bottom'.

The most distinctive mark of a grenadier, however, was the bearskin cap. At first the fur was built around a cap of red cloth 12 inches high. The red cloth was left exposed on top of the crown at the back of the cap. Later caps merely had red patches sewn to the fur. A shaped front plate carried the King's crest in white metal on a black ground with the motto 'NEC ASPERA TERRENT'. At the rear of the cap, on the fur, was a grenade motif in metal bearing the number of the regiment. The royal regiments and the six old corps were to have additional badges (see Appendix C) to be worn on the upper back part of the cap, ie, the red patch. These however were not always worn. There is also evidence that some regiments had no front plates at all, but this could be because of over-zealous officers ordering their grenadiers to cover their existing cloth mitre caps with fur until the official pattern was issued. Inspection returns show that for some considerable time after the 1768 warrant many grenadier

GRENADIER CAPS.
a. Pattern of front plate (after Warrant of 1768).
b. Rear of cap showing grenade badge and how hair queue is tucked under.
c. Cap plate of grenadiers of 37th Foot.
d. Cap plate of grenadiers of Marines.

EXAMPLES OF CARTRIDGE POUCH BADGES.
a. Foot Guards, found in New York City.
b. 45th Foot, found in New York City.
c. 15th Foot, found at White Plains, New York.

companies were without bearskin caps. It is more than likely that by the time the American War commenced the official bearskin cap was worn by most grenadiers. Some regiments, the 40th Foot for instance, had caps of white goatskin for the grenadier company (white caps were also worn by some musicians). By about 1778 it was becoming common practice for grenadiers to add white cords and tassels to the bearskin cap. These varied in style from one regiment to another but usually had the tassels hanging down on the right side. It was recommended that painted linen covers be worn over bearskin caps on the march to protect the fur. Like the cocked hats many bearskins had tapes sewn to the lining to tie under the hair for security. Grenadiers wore their hair braided in a plait which was powdered and tucked up under the cap. On field service many grenadiers wore the cocked hat in place of the bearskin as this was more suited to forest fighting. There are also records of leather caps of light infantry pattern with grenade badges on the front. This seems to indicate that in the interest of utility some grenadiers wore these on service.

Another distinguishing mark of the grenadier was a sword and a match case carried attached to the shoulder belt on the chest. The swords appear to have been rather unpopular. The Inspection Return for 42nd Foot of June 1769 states that the grenadiers declined to wear swords, preferring only the bayonet. This regiment, being a Highland corps, was equipped throughout with broadswords and it is known that these, along with pistols, were laid aside during the campaign of 1776. The match case, relic of earlier days when grenades were lit, was at this time purely decorative. After the war, in June 1784, a Council of General Officers recommended that the match cases and swords of the grenadiers should be abolished.

Finally, there is evidence of grenade badges being worn on the flap of some grenadier cartridge pouches in place of the regular regimental motif used by battalion men. These grenades were sometimes in metal and others were simply painted on.

LIGHT COMPANIES

By the time the American War began, the value of light infantry had already been established. Earlier campaigns in the Colonies had prompted the authorities to add a light infantry company to each of the marching regiments. Like the grenadier companies, the light companies were detached from their regiments and organized into provisional units for the duration of the war. They were always drawn up in two files with a distance of two feet between. Also, like the grenadiers, the light troops were considered something of an élite, being made up from the smaller, more agile men in the regiment.

The dress of the light infantry man differed considerably from that of his colleagues in the centre companies. The coat was cut short to form a jacket and, like the grenadiers', had shoulder wings. The tails of these jackets sometimes had lace patterns peculiar to the light companies or vertical rather than the usual horizontal pockets. Only the front flaps of the jacket were turned back. The light infantry also wore a distinctive red waistcoat sometimes braided with lace and sometimes without. There appear to have been exceptions even to this distinction. The Inspection Return for the 19th Foot for May 1775 states that the light company officers had white instead of red vests. Legwear was similar to that of the rest of the regiment. The original half-spatterdashes were of linen but these were discovered to be unsuitable for forest warfare so later half-gaiters were made of wool.

Light infantry headgear consisted of some form of small cap in place of the cocked hat. The official pattern was to be of black leather with three chains circling the crown and a metal fitting on top. It was to have a turned-up front peak bearing a crown above and the letters GR flanking the regimental number. There were, however, numerous variations of the cap. Apart from individual regimental patterns, many light troops cut down or turned up one side of their cocked hats. It became fashionable to decorate the caps with either a feather or an animal tail. Here again styles for this varied considerably. Light company men of some regiments wore red feathers in their caps as a mark of defiance to the American sharpshooters.

Equipment for the light companies was similar to that of the other troops but with certain additions. Belts are often shown as being of black leather. The waistbelt carried a frog for a hatchet as well as the bayonet and often held a small black leather cartridge box on the front carrying about nine rounds. Contemporary illustrations show this 'belly box' worn either with the usual hip pouch or instead of it. When the hatchet was not in use it was recommended that it be tied upon the knapsack. Light infantry were also equipped with powder horns and bullet bags but apparently these were worn so infrequently during the American War that a report of General Officers in June 1784 suggested they be laid aside. In place of the usual blanket, light troops were supplied with a grey 'maude' or woollen plaid. On campaign this was worn either 'en banderole' (across the body over the left shoulder, tied on the right hip) or slung over the shoulders.

The light infantry firearm was a fusil or fusee, shorter and lighter than the standard infantry musket. A small number of light infantry men were armed with the excellent Ferguson rifle, a weapon named after its inventor, Patrick Ferguson, an officer of the 71st Foot. The Ferguson had a screw plug at the breech which could be opened to insert a charge by one turn of the trigger guard. It was claimed that a soldier trained in the use of this weapon could fire six shots per minute from a standing position. The rifle had an overall length of 52 inches (36-inch barrel length). With Captain Ferguson's death at King's Mountain in 1780 efforts to further the issue of the weapon lapsed and this, coupled with petty differences in the British High Command, resulted in the project being discarded.

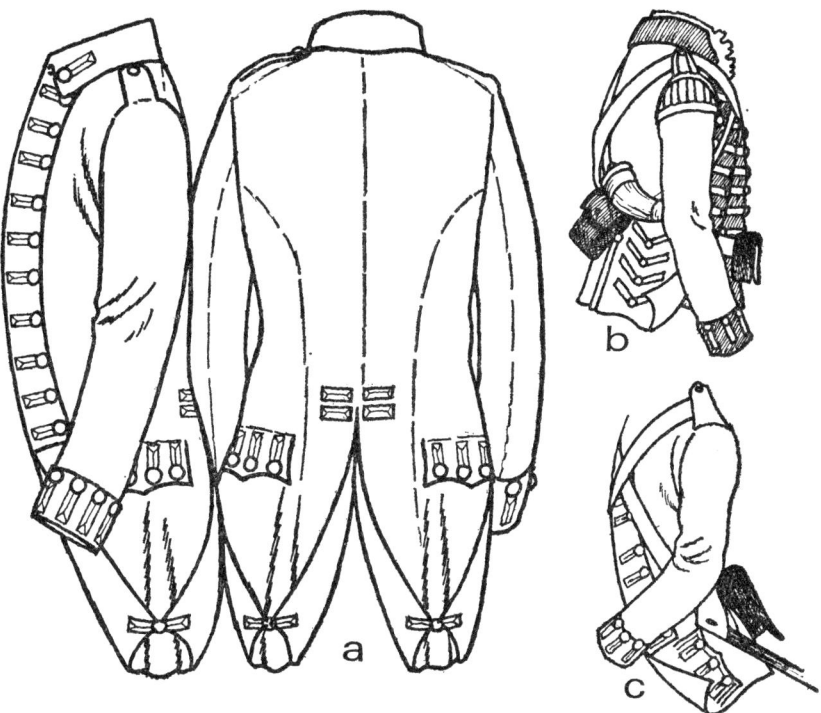

INFANTRY COAT PATTERNS.
a. Side and rear views of Private's coat (*battalion company*).
b. Short light infantry coat showing pocket variation.
c. Light infantry coat of the 62nd Foot.

OFFICERS

Officers' coats were basically the same in style as those of the rank and file although the fabric and cut would be of finer quality. In an officer corps with a high proportion of wealthy members, it is understandable that many of the whims and affectations of costume evident in civilian fashions would be reflected in the dress of affluent officers. Utility also played a part in officers' uniforms. Like the men, many appear to have cut down their coats to waist length. This is illustrated on at least two officers in Graham's painting of the death of General Frazer.

On service, lapels were frequently worn buttoned across the chest or unbuttoned altogether as well as buttoned back in the fashion most represented by painters. Buttons were silver or gilt and any lace or epaulette corresponded in colour. Colonels decided whether metallic lace should be worn around the buttonholes or not and in the American War many officers either substituted white lace or omitted the lace altogether. This, of course, was an attempt to avoid becoming the prime targets of American marksmen.

Another coat similar in cut to the full regimentals and called a 'frock' uniform was frequently worn by officers. This was usually devoid of part or all of the ace and was often without cuff buttons.

LIGHT INFANTRY COAT AND CAP.
a. Light Infantry coat of the 69th Foot.
b. The rather curious light infantry company cap of the 69th Foot. The black cap has a black feather. Trimming and insignia are white. The man's hair is braided and tucked under the cap in grenadier fashion.

Battalion company officers wore a single epaulette on the right shoulder while officers of flank companies wore one on each, often with the addition of laced shoulder wings. Styles of officers' epaulettes varied considerably. Many were made up from a strip of lace worked into a decorative knot while others were simple with a regimental device upon them. Still others were made from cloth in the facing colour edged with silver or gilt lace or braid.

Officers on duty were also supposed to wear a crescent-shaped piece of metal at the throat called a gorget. This was a reminder of the days of plate armour and was suspended around the neck on a ribbon. At this time these were usually silver (occasionally gilt), and bore the Royal Arms and the regimental number. Some also carried the badge of the regiment.

Like the coat lace, gorgets were often laid aside by officers on campaign who considered them too much of an identification mark. It is known, however, that they were worn by many officers at Bunker Hill.

To return to the coats; turnbacks were held, like those of the men, by a bow of embroidery or lace. Other fasteners included metal hearts or grenades.

Another distinguishing mark of an officer was a crimson silk sash worn around the waist under the coat and knotted on the left side.

Small clothes (waistcoat and breeches) were white or buff (for buff facings). Waistcoats were fastened either with a single or double row of small regimental buttons down the front and usually had two horizontal pockets. Occasionally the waistcoat was laced but this was uncommon. Light company officers were supposed to wear red waistcoats (more frequently laced) but many wore white.

Breeches were worn either with spatterdashes or knee boots (often of the jockey type). On campaign many officers wore overalls like their men, or Indian leggings.

Sword belts, at first worn around the waist and then over the right shoulder under the coat, were almost all worn over the coat by the end of 1775. They were at first fastened in the centre of the chest by a buckle of the colour of the button metal but soon these were replaced by a rectangular or oval plate engraved with the device of the regiment. The sword belt, about 2 inches wide, was of white or buff leather. Officers of flank companies also wore a second belt over the left shoulder carrying the cartridge pouch.

LIGHT INFANTRY CAPS.
a. 45th Foot. Officers. Silver trim. Green plume.
b. Regulation pattern of Light Company cap. White metal trim. Black turban and plume.
c. 62nd Foot. White star. Brass comb. Red crest.
d. 7th Foot (Royal Fusiliers). White star. Fur crest.
e. 5th Foot. White metal fittings. Red turban and horsehair crest.
f. Marines. White metal plate (background black). Red crown with white lace.
g. 71st Foot. Black velvet turban. Badge and chain design in white. Sometimes had black ostrich plume from black cockade.

OFFICERS (from contemporary sources).
a. Officer of the 4th Foot.
b. Lord Petersham. Grenadier Coy. of 29th Foot.
c. Colonel St. Leger. 34th Foot.
  Note white fur shabraque with metallic crest and trim. These became fashionable for officers of foot regiments.
  In all three cases the officers' coats are devoid of lace.

EPAULETTES.
Examples of the many variations of epaulette worn by officers.

It was specified that the swords of each regiment were to be of a uniform pattern, with either gilt or silver hilts matching the button metal. Sword knots were of metallic thread worked with crimson.

A pole weapon called a spontoon was carried by battalion company officers. These were to prove too cumbersome for field operations in America and were soon discarded. Officers of grenadier and light companies were armed with fusils.

GORGETS, AND POLE WEAPONS.
a. Front and side views. 14th Foot. Silver.
b. 42nd Foot (Royal Highland Regiment). Silver.
c. Sergeant's Halberd.
d. Officers' Espontoons.

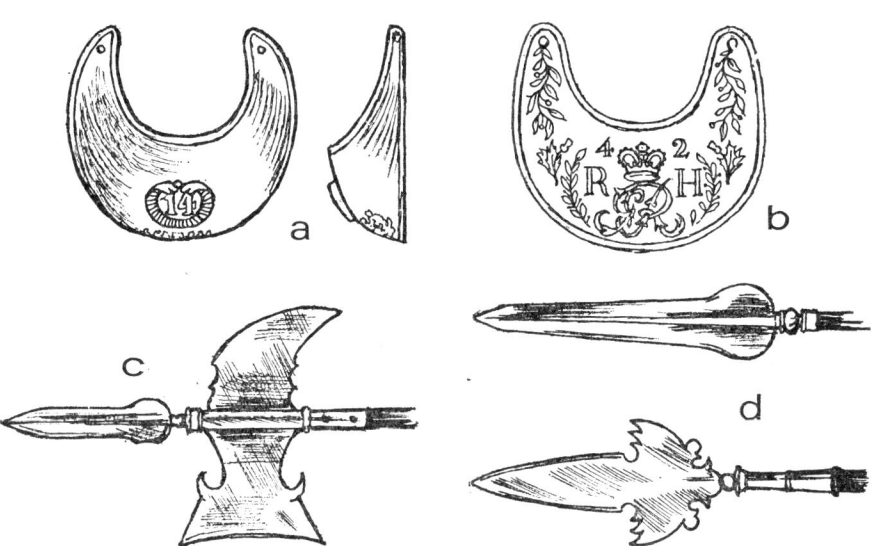

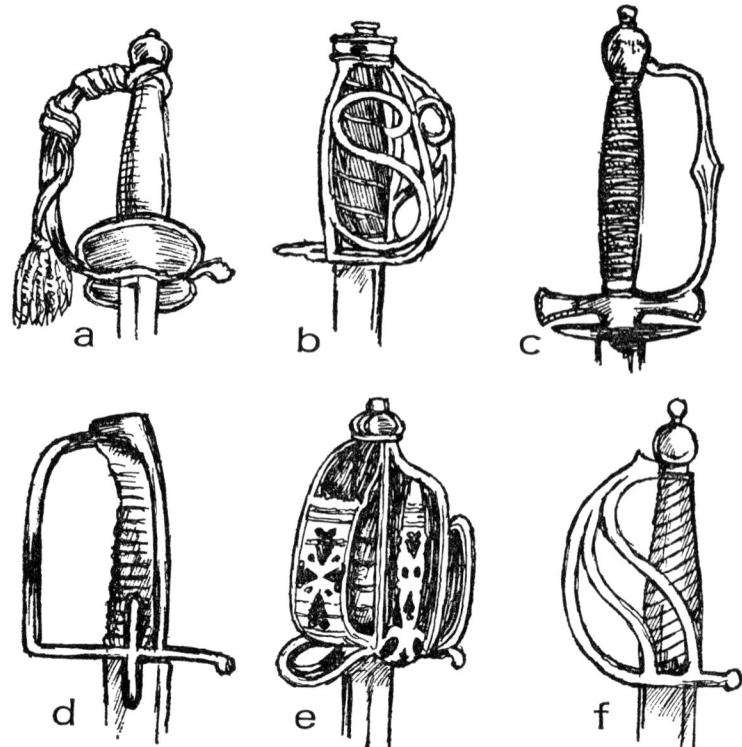

TYPES OF SWORD HILT.
a. Infantry Officers. Regulation sword. 32 in. blade. Crimson and Gilt tasselled knot.
b. Type of Grenadier's hilt. Regimental patterns varied.
c. Individual regimental pattern. 35th Foot.
d. Typical Light Dragoon hilt of the period. 31 in. blade.
e. Typical hilt of Highland broadsword.
f. Another type of Grenadier hanger hilt. 27 in. blade.

Head-dress of officers followed the style of that of the men. Battalion company officers wore cocked hats edged with gold or silver lace (often removed on field service) and frequently left the tassels of the tightening cords hanging over the brim. The hats had a black cockade with a regimental button and a loop matching the coat lace.

Officers of grenadier companies wore the black bearskin cap with the same design as their men in silver on a blackened front plate. Some wore white or metallic cords and tassels hanging down on the right side of the cap.

Light company officers adopted a similar type of cap to their men although the embellishments were usually more elaborate than those of the rank and file.

Mounted officers of infantry usually had plain saddles, although some had saddle cloths in the facing colour of the regiment (as specified for Majors and Adjutants) edged with metallic lace and perhaps bearing the regiment's badge or number. By the middle of the war sheepskin or white fur shabraques became fashionable, again trimmed with metallic lace and bearing a badge in the rear corners.

GENERAL OFFICERS

The coat usually worn by General Officers at this period was the 'frock'. This was, in fact, the second uniform but was worn on most dress occasions. It was made of scarlet cloth with dark blue lapels and round cuffs. The coat had no collar (except a small stand-up one of scarlet with a lace and button on each side) or turnbacks but was cut away on the slope down the front edges. It had laced pockets and was lined white. The buttons were gilt bearing a crossed sword and baton design and the gilt buttonhole lace was of a special 'chain' pattern. Gilt epaulettes were worn on either one or both shoulders having no link with rank scales. Waistcoat and breeches were white after 1772 but there is evidence that many Generals wore buff small clothes and linings.

Generals also wore a uniform like that described above but with simpler lace of silk twist in place of the chain pattern.

For grand occasions a third coat, the 'uniform' coat, was worn. This had no collar or lapels but carried large gilt embroidery around the coat edges and blue cuffs. The waistcoat was also embroidered.

For Generals, buttons were set singly, for Major-Generals in twos and for Lieutenant-Generals in threes.

The cuffs of the 'uniform' coat had no buttons and bore one lace ring for Major-Generals and two for Lieutenant-Generals.

Specifications of 1769 state that Adjutant-Generals and Quartermaster-Generals were to have a red coat without collar, faced blue with silver laced buttonholes and buttons set in threes.

Deputy Adjutant-Generals and Deputy Quartermaster-Generals were similarly dressed but with buttons set in twos.

These same ranks for particular commands were dressed as above but with one epaulette on the right shoulder for infantry and one on the left for cavalry.

NON-COMMISSIONED OFFICERS

Narrow silver lace was specified for Sergeant-Majors and Sergeants wore plain white lace. They wore a worsted waist sash of crimson with a centre stripe of the facing colour. Sergeants of regiments with red facings had a white central stripe on the sash.

Battalion company sergeants were to carry halberds (a pole weapon with a decorative head) but like the spontoons of the officers these were laid aside in favour of firearms in America. Officially battalion company sergeants were to wear no pouch belts but if using firearms obviously did. Cocked hats of sergeants were laced silver. Sergeants of grenadier and light company carried fusils and pouches. All sergeants were to carry swords although again this often proved impracticable during the American War.

Corporals wore their rank badge on the right shoulder, either in the form of a looped and tasselled cord or a white silk fringed epaulette. Hat lace for corporals was white.

DRUMMERS AND FIFERS

Drummers and fifers were to be of a 'genteel appearance' and it was recommended that the age of fourteen was the best time to commence training.

Although the Clothing Warrant of 1768 states clearly the pattern of coat for drummers and fifers, many individual regimental patterns existed. In fact, many officers made it their business to see that the musicians of the regiment were

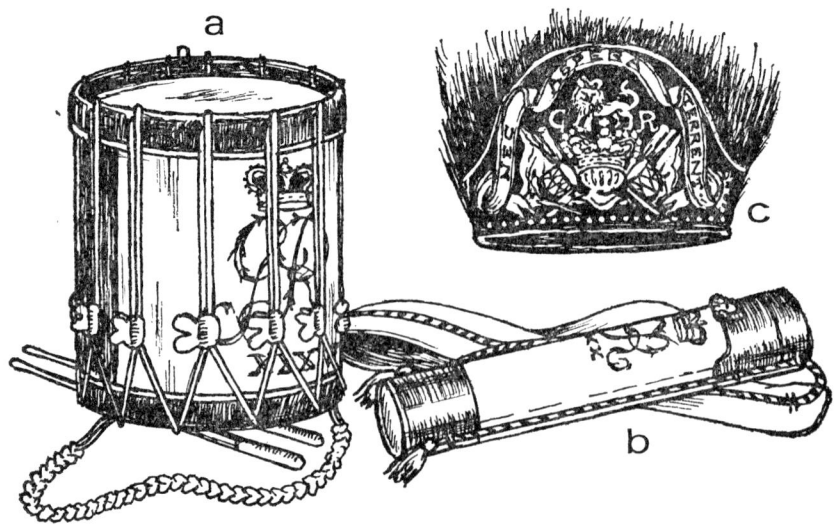

INFANTRY MUSIC.
a. Side drum. Front half painted in facing colour with Royal cypher, crown and regimental number below.
b. Fife case. Painted in facing colour with metal fittings. Often the shoulder belt carrying the cord was omitted and case was slung from cord only.
c. Musician's cap plate.

well furnished with attractive uniforms. The 'music' led a regiment on the march and it was no doubt considered that it would give an imposing effect to onlookers if the players were decoratively clothed.

Officially the coats of drummers and fifers of royal regiments were to be red, lined white with blue facings and 'royal' lace (yellow with a blue stripe). They wore white waistcoats and breeches.

Those regiments whose facings were red clothed their drummers in white coats, faced and lined with red. These musicians wore red waistcoats and breeches.

The remainder of the regiments were to dress their drummers and fifers in coats of the facing colour, faced red and lined white. Any regiments with buff facings clothed their musicians in buff coats, faced and lined red with red waistcoats and breeches.

Although some regiments had black facings, no illustrations ever show black coats for their drummers. It is likely that these were worn, however, as a King's approval of November 1780 states that drummers' coats were changed from 'black to white cloth'.

Lace for all but the royal regiments was of the regimental pattern. Apart from the buttonholes, lace was usually arranged on the seams of the coat with six lace chevrons on the sleeves. Some contemporary illustrations show these with points uppermost whilst others show points downward. According to the 1768 Warrant the Colonel of a regiment decided on the style of lacing. All the coats had laced shoulder wings.

Caps were of black bearskin, similar to those of grenadiers but having trophies of colours and drums flanking the King's crest on the front plate.

The back of the cap was to bear the regiment's number and any badge a regiment was entitled to wear. Some illustrations show a drum badge on the fur at the back of the cap. The recommended black bearskin cap for drummers and fifers was not always worn. A number of regiments favoured caps of white goatskin or fur and cocked hats are often shown, either feathered or plain.

All drummers and fifers carried a short scimitar bladed sword, at first hanging from a waistbelt and later from a belt over the right shoulder.

Drums were made of wood with the hoops usually in red and the front half of the shell painted the regiments facing colour with a crown and royal cypher in gold. Below this was the regiment's number in white Roman numerals. Drum cords were white.

Regiments with special badges carried these on the drum shells in place of the cypher. Fife cases were either of painted wood with metal fittings or all metal. They were decorated in a similar fashion to the drums and were carried on the right hip hanging from a cord (sometimes this was on a white belt) over the left shoulder.

Drum Majors wore an ornamental belt over the right shoulder which carried a pair of silver mounted drumsticks on the chest. Their coats might be as ornate as the Colonel allowed.

MUSICIANS

A great number of the musicians who made up the regimental bands were foreigners. Bands at this time consisted of anything between eight musicians and twice that number. The instrumentation was very limited being composed usually only of oboes, clarinets, horns and bassoons. No percussion instruments were included although sometimes 'clash pans' (cymbals) were used.

It is impossible to give accurate descriptions of the dress of these musicians so varied were their costumes. In general coats were heavily laced and hats dressed with feathers and plumes.

FUSILIERS

Three regiments of fusiliers took part in the American War, the 7th (Royal Fusiliers), the 21st (Royal North British Fusiliers) and the 23rd (Royal Welsh Fusiliers).

They were clothed similarly to the other Line regiments but with the battalion company men wearing black bearskin caps instead of cocked hats. The fusilier caps specified in the 1768 Warrant were to be not so high as those ordered for grenadiers and to be without the grenade motif on the back. As the Warrant does not make mention of light companies of fusilier regiments it is not stated whether or not bearskin caps were also intended for them. It would seem unlikely when one remembers their function.

There is some confusion in the evidence regarding the wearing of fusilier caps in America. The 7th in 1770 are recorded as having 'good caps' but not of bearskin or according to regulation. It could be, however, that they had received them by the time the war commenced. Certainly drawings of 1788 show bearskins. Inspection returns of the 7th frequently mentions 'helmets'. It is not known whether this refers to the head-dress of the light company only

COATS AND WINTER CLOTHING.

a. Front and rear views of Musician's coat.

b. Rear view of Light Dragoon coat.

c. Rear view of winter capote—light blue trim. (See also colour plate on page 37.)

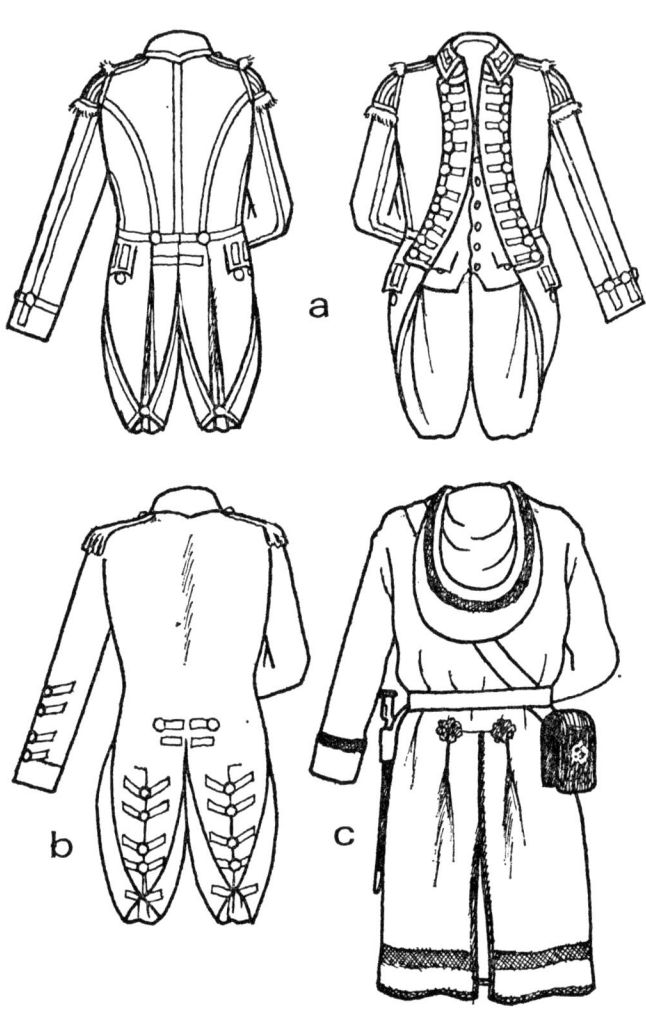

or if all companies wore helmets to preserve the bearskin caps for parades.

An example of a light company style cap of the 7th Foot found in America is very similar in shape to those shown in illustrations of the Regiment in 1789 although rather more basic. Inspection Returns of 1774 for the 21st Foot specify 'new caps' and the 1784 Return mentions 'bearskin caps'.

Apparently the 23rd Foot were not so fortunate. Their Returns for 1770 state that caps of the old pattern were still in use (presumably cloth) and in 1794 'neither officers or men had their fusilier caps'. In this latter case the capmaker had failed to deliver on time. It is, of course, probable that the Regiment had been equipped with fur caps in time for the American War. The light company cap of the 23rd in 1771 was a black leather cap with a red turned-up front peak and a turban of black silk. The cap was surmounted with a black fur crest and had a white plume on the left side. (Although not mentioned it probably had the Regiment's badge or number on the red peak.) Officers and Sergeants of fusilier regiments carried fusils.

Mention should be made here of the caps of the 5th Foot (later the Northumberland Fusiliers). Although at the time of their service in America they were not a fusilier regiment, the grenadiers and battalion companies all wore bearskin caps. Grenadiers were distinguished by their match-cases on the pouch belt. The light company of the 5th wore a distinctive leather cap, an example of which survives today.

PIONEERS

Pioneers wore caps with black leather crowns which had black fur upright fronts. On these fronts was a small red turn-up flap with a crossed saw and axe badge. These men wore heavy brown leather aprons. They were equipped with saws and axes in leather cases.

HIGHLAND REGIMENTS

At the outbreak of the American War the 42nd Foot (Black Watch) was the only regiment in the British Army wearing Highland dress. As the war progressed, however, it was necessary to raise more troops and a great many of these came from Scotland. It is not necessary to name these new bodies here as they are dealt with later on in the section of the book which lists all of the regiments which served in America.

The dress of the Highland troops was based on that of the other Line infantry, but as in the past, incorporated features of Scottish national costume.

The coats were red, faced as usual, with the buttonholes laced and having a white lining. They were shorter than those worn by the English regiments and had only the front skirts turned back. The regular distinctions for grenadiers and light company men, such as shoulder wings, were observed (although unlike the other light infantry men the Highlanders wore white waistcoats). Buttons were pewter. Sergeants' lace was silver but was usually removed on campaign. That mark of the Highland soldier of the 18th century, the belted plaid (breacan-an-feileadh) was still worn although now made of less material than before. Alternatively many contemporary illustrations show the little kilt (feilidh beag) being worn. The basic tartan pattern of almost all Highland regiments was the 'Government sett'. This was dark in colour based on a pattern of black, blue and green. It was what is known today as the 'Black Watch' tartan, being worn by this Regiment as well as a number of others. There is evidence that some regiments used this sett with the addition of lines

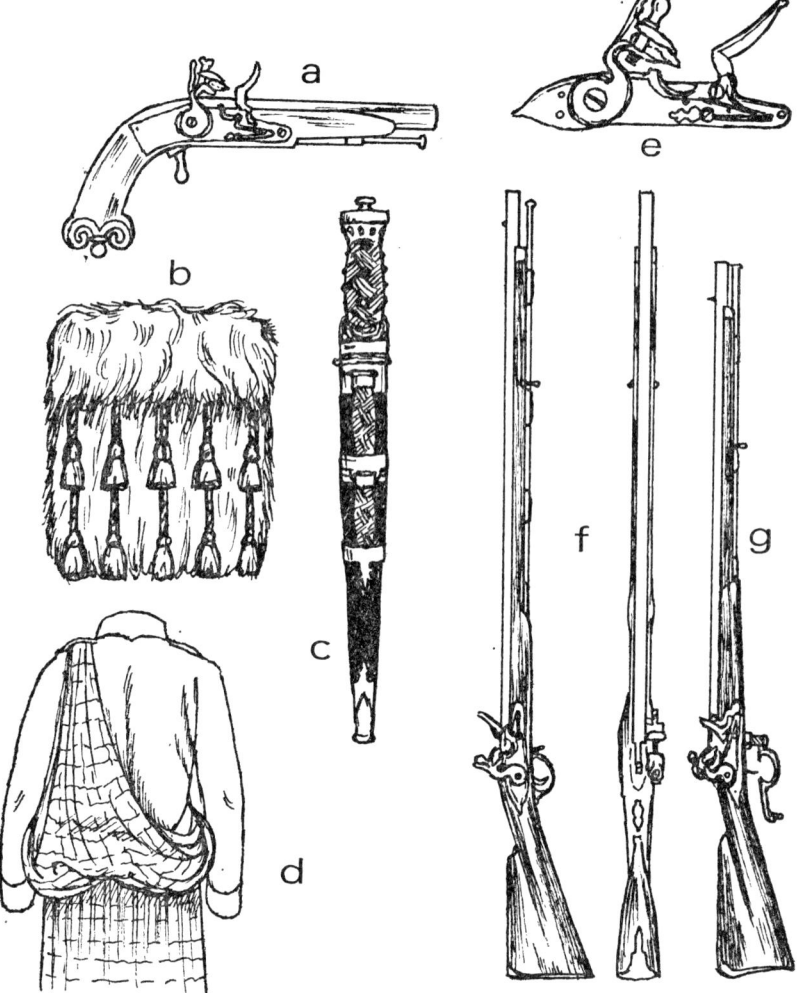

EQUIPMENT DETAILS.
a. Highland 'Ramshorn' pistol. Stock and butt gun-metal. Barrel steel.
b. Sporran of 71st Highlanders. (Grey fur, white tassels, red bells.)
c. Officer's dirk (from a specimen at Fort Ticonderoga).
d. Rear view of the belted plaid. Tied up at shoulder.
e. Lock detail of the Brown Bess musket.
f. Side and plan views of the Brown Bess musket.
g. The Ferguson rifle with screw breech open.

of one or more colour. Details are scanty and it is impossible for hard and fast rules to be laid down regarding all the differences in the tartans employed. Colonel's choice, fading and colour changes through wear, availability etc, all would contribute to how a regiment would appear on service.

Drummers and fifers appear to have worn a variation or in some cases a totally different tartan from the rank and file. This was usually a red based tartan similar to the Stewart sett, which became known as the 'Music Tartan'. Diced patterns of various designs were also used on the stockings of Highlanders.

The designs are always shown as diagonal, usually red and white checks finely outlined with black. Occasionally a green check may be found in them. Red garters with bows were worn and shoes were black leather with metal buckles.

Sporran patterns also varied, the most usual for the men being white goatskin and buff leather. At this time Highlanders wore belts of black leather in place of the usual white or buff. The broadsword which was worn by all, including battalion company men, was soon discarded as being an unsuitable weapon. Even before arrival in America the Scots had put off their swords in favour of the bayonet only. Like swords the all-metal pistols which were at this time carried by Highlanders were laid aside. Neither sword nor pistol were ever again taken into use by the rank and file. The smaller cartridge pouch was often worn as a 'belly box' on the front of a waist belt rather than the larger one on the shoulder belt.

Unlike the rest of the Line regiments, the Highland battalion company men did not wear the cocked hat. Their headgear was the Kilmarnock bonnet. This was made of blue cloth, sometimes stiffened with a red tourie on top and a diced band of red, white and green around. The black cockade on the left side held a tuft of black feathers which lay over the cap. More feathers were added as time went on until, by the end of the 18th century the bonnets were so heavy with feathers that they began to take on the appearance of fur caps.

The 71st Highlanders are reputed to have worn a red feather as a mark of defiance but this is not shown in contemporary pictures.

Grenadier companies followed the normal system of wearing the bearskin

HIGHLAND REGIMENT DETAILS.
a. Shoulder belt plate. Royal Highland Emigrants.
b. Other ranks' button. Royal Highland Emigrants. Pewter.
c. Officer's button. Royal Highland Emigrants. Gilt.
d. Other ranks' button. 42nd Foot (found in America). Pewter.
e. 71st Foot. Officer's in silver, men's pewter. (Note figure 1 stamped back to front.)   f. Officer's button. Royal Edinburgh Volunteers. Silver.
g. Other rank's button. Royal Edinburgh Volunteers. Pewter.
h. Bonnet badge. 71st Foot. Silver.

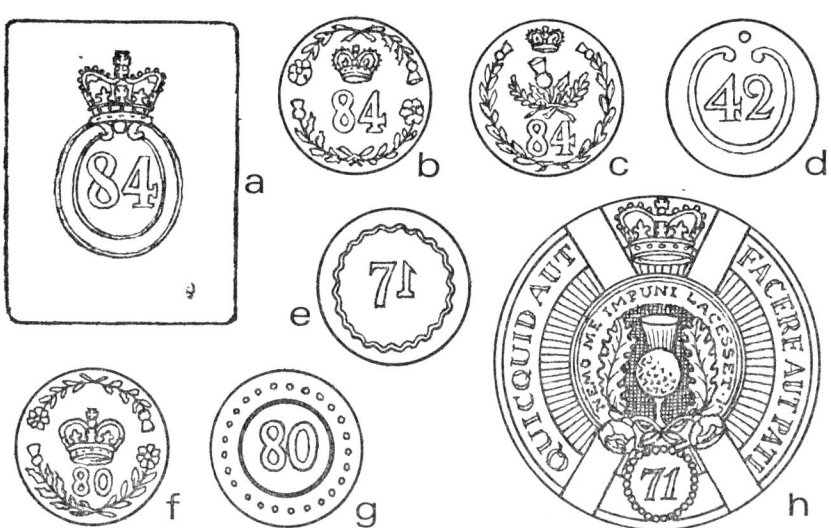

cap with the usual trimmings, while light companies wore leather helmets of the regimental pattern. It appears that the light company of the 42nd wore the blue bonnets like battalion men.

Having described the imposing appearance of a Highland soldier in full dress it must now be added that within a short time of experiencing service in North America, the Scottish image had all but disappeared. Like the sword and pistol, the kilt, after being worn in some early actions was laid aside as being totally unsuitable for the American campaign. For the men, it was replaced by white breeches fashioned from the canvas of old tents and worn with short black cloth gaiters. The overalls of various hues worn by the English regiments were also adopted by many Scots.

An early attempt at camouflage was even made with the white parts of the uniform being stained with earth dyes to cut down glare. Tomahawks were now widely carried by men of grenadier, battalion and light companies.

The blue bonnet of the battalion men was virtually all that remained to identify the Highland regiments.

HIGHLAND OFFICERS

Dressed similarly to their men, Highland officers had certain uniform distinctions not worn by English Line officers. They wore two epaulettes rather than one and the crimson sash was worn over the left shoulder (tied on the right hip) instead of around the waist. This was supposedly to keep it clear of the large basket hilt of the broadsword. Buttonholes were laced with gold or silver lace although, as usual, this was very often removed on campaign.

Most contemporary evidence shows officers' sporrans as being brown fur with white or silver tassel decorations. One portrait of an officer of the light company of the 42nd shows white breeches with knee length gaiters. He wears a short coat laced with gold and gold epaulettes with wings (somewhat unusual for this early period). His hat is the blue bonnet with black feathers. Many officers at this time wore white sword belts in place of black although this was not general practice for the men until almost the end of the century. Spontoons were laid aside and fusils were carried by the officers.

FOOT GUARDS

A battalion composed of drafts from each of the three Guards regiments was created on February 13th, 1776. It embarked for America in April of the same year under Colonel William Mather of the Coldstream Guards. As commander of this composite unit Mather was ranked as Brigadier.

One company each of grenadiers and light infantrymen were made up from the Guards. The proportions of men from each regiment in these companies was:

	Sergeants	Corporals	Men
From the 1st Foot Guards	2	2	42
From the Coldstream Guards	1	1	27
From the 3rd Foot Guards	1	1	27

Although serving as a single battalion the Guards of each regiment retained their own uniform. Like the Line regiments the uniforms of the Foot Guards were to undergo considerable changes following the 1768 Clothing Warrant. Further alterations were made before their involvement in the American War.

1st REGIMENT OF FOOT GUARDS (after 1770)

The coat was similar to that of the Line regiments with the addition of more white lace. The coat was lined white with shoulder straps, collar, lapels and

Left to right: BATTALION COMPANY PRIVATE OF THE 42nd FOOT (CAMPAIGN DRESS).

GRENADIER COMPANY OFFICER OF THE 71st FOOT.

BATTALION COMPANY PRIVATE OF THE 84th FOOT (ROYAL HIGHLAND EMIGRANTS).

round cuffs in blue all laced white. The lace loops (with pewter buttons) were diamond shaped and were placed four on each cuff, ten on each lapel (equally spaced) four on each pocket flap (which was also edged around with white lace) and two on each side of the rear vent which was also edged in lace. Strips of lace also ran from the bottom of the lapels to the hem and from the rear of the pockets down to the hem at the back. These would scarcely be seen when the turnbacks were fastened up. The buttons were flat. Waistcoat and breeches were white without lace. White gaiters were worn in parade dress according to old prints. Grenadiers had blue shoulder-wings laced white and the light company had the same (with coats shortened to jackets).

Cocked hats were edged with white lace and the fur caps of the grenadiers bore the Royal Arms in white metal on a black background. A portrait of an officer of the Guards light company painted in America in 1776 shows the cap as a black hat with a small curly brim decorated on the left side with a white feather.

Sergeants were similarly dressed with gilt buttons and lace until March 1776 when Brigade Orders gave permission for them to substitute white lace in place of gilt. They were also ordered to lay aside their halberds and to be armed with fusils for the campaign. Corporals wore silk epaulettes.

Drummers wore a red coat lined white and laced with white silk lace with 'tinsel' stripes. Collar and diamond looped shoulder-wings were trimmed with white silk fringe. Waistcoat and breeches were white and fur caps were worn.

COLDSTREAM REGIMENT OF FOOT GUARDS (after 1773)

Dress as for the 1st Guards with the following differences: Distinctions on the coat included ten buttons set in twos on 'scallop-headed' (pointed) white lace loops on the lapel. Four in twos on each cuff and pocket. Grenadiers' shoulder-wings were blue like the rest of the facings, and were edged and looped with six white laces in twos and fringed. They had blue-edged white shoulder-straps. As with the 1st Guards the collar, lapels, cuffs and edges of the coat were laced white. Grenadier cap plates had a background of red instead of black. Sergeants are listed as having a gold epaulette. Drummers were dressed similarly to privates with the addition of six sleeve chevron laces (points downward), blue shoulder wings cross barred with lace and fringed. The cuffs had four laces and buttons in twos and the body laced 'state fashion instead of common straight lace'.

3rd REGIMENT OF FOOT GUARDS (after 1774)

The Clothing Warrant of 1768 had specified similar lacing to the Coldstream Guards for the 3rd Guards. Alterations of July 1774, however, had provided the 3rd with a distinct pattern which was worn in time for the American campaign.

The red coats were lined white and faced blue with nine buttons on pointed white laces set in threes on each lapel. Each cuff, pocket and back skirt had three loops of white lace. Grenadiers' wings were looped in two sets of three laces. The bearskin caps had all white metal front plates.

Sergeants, according to the 1768 Warrant, were to have a gold fringed epaulette lined blue (grenadier sergeants two epaulettes) and gold lace. This lace would be changed for white in America (Brigade Orders, March 1776). Corporals in 1768 are stated as having blue collar, cuffs, epaulettes and shoulder straps laced with silver, also blue lapels laced with white worsted. White lace was probably used throughout by 1776.

Drummers, from 1768, were to have a white coat with blue lining, collar, cuffs, lapels and wings white laced around and also down the seams, sleeves, sides and skirts. Waistcoats were to be red bound with lace and breeches white. White fur caps with yellow front plates were ordered.

As will be seen, exact details of the dress of the Guards battalion in America are vague. Little is known of the light companies and even the uniforms of the officers are not well documented. Like the sergeants they were permitted by the Brigade Order of March 1776 to use white lace in place of gold and to carry fusils in place of spontoons. It seems likely that the gold lace was removed from their hats and that gorgets were laid aside.

Like officers of the Line they wore the crimson waist-sash.

MARINES

An extract of Marine battalion orders of May 1775 reads as follows: 'The right honourable the lords commissioners of the Admiralty, having directed a re-inforcement of Marines to serve under Major Pitcairne in General Gage's army, consisting of 2 Majors, 10 Captains, 27 Subalterns, 2 Adjutants, 1 Surgeon, 2 Assistant-Surgeons, 28 Sergeants, 25 Corporals, 20 Drummers, 600 Privates, the Commanding Officer deems it necessary for the good of the service to form the whole under his command into 2 battalions.' In each battalion (1st and 2nd) are 8 companies plus grenadiers and light infantry (3 officers to each company).

Marines were in Boston at the outbreak of the war and served at Lexington, Bunker Hill and Quebec. Although posted to Halifax, Nova Scotia, detachments of Marines served elsewhere throughout the war. In the Line the Marines ranked between the 49th and 50th Foot regiments.

Marines were dressed in a similar fashion to the Line regiments. Their red coats were faced white (collar, cuffs, lapels and turn-backs). The pewter buttons bore an anchor device and although officially the lace was 'blue with

MARINE DETAILS.
a. *Marine officer's gorget. Silver.*
b. *Other ranks' button. Pewter.*
c. *Officer's button. Silver.*
d. and e. *Two designs of officers' silver shoulder belt plates.*

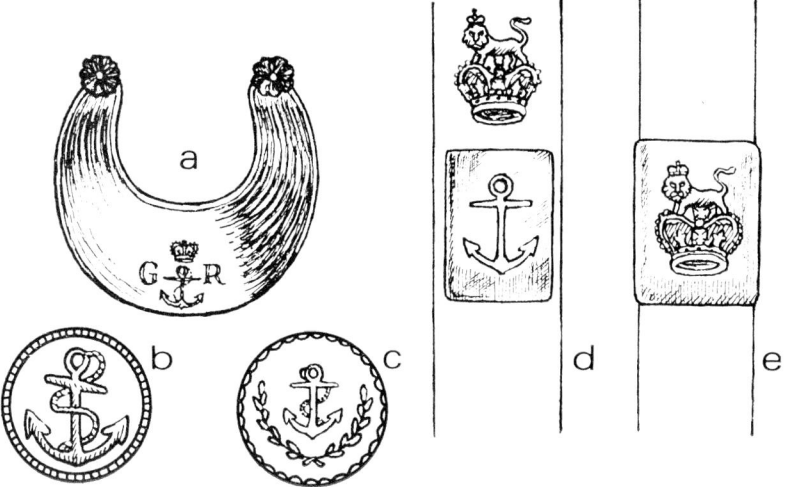

Left to right: BATTALION COMPANY CORPORAL OF THE COLDSTREAM GUARDS (CAMPAIGN DRESS).

GRENADIER COMPANY MAN OF THE 3rd FOOT GUARDS (FULL DRESS).

BATTALION COMPANY OFFICER OF THE 1st GUARDS.

Left to right: *LIGHT COMPANY OFFICER OF THE 42nd FOOT (FROM A CONTEMPORARY ILLUSTRATION).*

INFANTRYMAN IN WINTER CAMPAIGN DRESS.

LIGHT COMPANY OFFICER OF THE 1st FOOT GUARDS (FROM A CONTEMPORARY ILLUSTRATION).

At Bunker Hill in 1775, one of the first major actions of the war, the British forces under General Gage concentrated all the Grenadier and Light Companies from several regiments into one composite force for greater shock effect. This painting by J. Trumbull shows the furious fighting around the earthworks of the hill which were to cause such heavy British casualties (NAM).

This water colour by Simkin depicts Grenadiers of the Line Regiments storming Bunker Hill and gives a good view of their uniform although it seems unlikely that they would have been wearing their knapsacks in action (NAM).

Left to right: LIGHT COMPANY OFFICER OF THE 10th FOOT.

BATTALION COMPANY SERGEANT OF THE 5th FOOT (CLOTHED AS FUSILIERS).

BATTALION COMPANY PRIVATE OF THE 27th FOOT (INNISKILLING REGIMENT).

Left to right: BATTALION COMPANY OFFICER OF MARINES.

LIGHT INFANTRYMAN IN CAMPAIGN DRESS
(FROM A CONTEMPORARY ILLUSTRATION).

DRUMMER OF THE 24th FOOT.

a red worm', it is very rarely shown on contemporary illustrations.

Grenadiers wore the usual distinctions of shoulder wings and match-cases. Light company men wore short coats (this is recorded as early as 1772). An order of February 1775 instructed that the men were to have long leather gaiters with buttons and also short ones. All were to have knapsacks and velvet stocks (fastened with a buckle for grenadiers and a clasp for the rest). In December of the same year it was ordered that the clothing was to be 'fitted by companies, no man to come on parade without laced hat, black stock and leggings'. It is interesting to note that despite the privations of campaign, the men were expected to parade as usual.

Halifax 1776 – prior to an inspection of both battalions, Captains were to see that men had 'clean shirt a with frill to it, a good black stock and half-gaiters. Pouches shining and polished.'

Headgear for the battalion company men was the usual cocked hat laced white with a black leather cockade and pewter button with anchor design. The hats of the grenadiers were recorded in 1771 as being cocked with no lace, with white looping and two white tassels on the right side. Later, grenadiers were issued with a black fur cap of the pattern specified for the infantry but with a distinctive Marine design on the front plate.

These fur caps were dispatched to the Officer commanding the Marines at Boston so it is debatable whether they would have arrived in time for Bunker Hill.

Light company men also wore a special cap with an anchor design on the front plate.

Battalion company sergeants (officially) carried halberds and flank company sergeants fusils.

OFFICERS

The dress of officers of Marines closely followed that of line officers but with their badges bearing the anchor motif. Their lace was silver but frequently removed altogether in America. Buttons and cap plates (flank companies) were silver. In February 1775, officers in America were ordered to 'provide themselves with long, leather gaiters with Hessian tops'.

In 1776 it was directed that officers of the 1st Battalion were to wear white gorget roses (ribbon decorations on the ends of the gorget), and short clubbed hair when under arms. Contemporary portraits also show black rosettes on gorgets, presumably for the 2nd Battalion. Gorgets were silver decorated with an inscribed anchor motif, crown and cypher.

In 1779 it was ordered that 'no black belts were to be worn except by flank company officers. Officers to wear laced coats and waistcoats.' Cross-belts and uniform swords were to be worn on all occasions.

Information for Marine officers in 1773 regarding dress on guard and general field days was as follows: Uniform coat, white waistcoat and breeches. Silver laced hat with silver band and looping. Black stock, black silk buckle gaiters. Sash, gorget, uniform sword and knot, half-gaiters except where long ones are ordered. Shoulder sword belt with clasp. Belt and pouch to be worn over coat as privates. Battalion officers hair queued, light and grenadier companies plaited and tucked.

A portrait of an officer of this period shows the hilt of the sword as having a lion head pommel with the stirrup bar in the mouth.

Marines are said to have carried colours at the Bunker Hill action but no details of these exist. Fragments of these colours were sold at Christies in 1912.

3: Artillery Uniforms

A COMPLETE description of the ordnance used by the Royal Artillery is outside the scope of this book, as it is limited to the coverage of the uniforms of the period, and I therefore refer the interested reader to the various specialized works on the subject.

Infantry regiments were usually accompanied by their own light guns, invariably 1½ or 3 pounders. Crews of Royal Artillery men were attached to the various regiments to operate these 'battalion guns'. This often meant, however, that the gunners were absent from their own Corps for some considerable time, a situation which caused not a little unrest and resulted in them being withdrawn by the end of the 18th century, leaving the infantry to operate their own guns.

At this time contractors with civilian teams were still employed to move the guns around, although it will be appreciated that in the American War these civilian handlers were not so easy to come by or particularly reliable. The drivers usually wore a white farm type smock or similar garment with either a cocked hat or jockey cap of leather or felt. They occasionally carried short swords but had, in the main, the appearance of civilians.

By the commencement of the American War the Royal Artillery was made up of four battalions. Although artillery served in numerous engagements throughout the war, the terrain did not permit the unimpeded movement of guns and wagons. Shortage of draught horses and accurate maps harassed the artillery officer at every turn. It was a situation in which gunners found themselves caught up in what was principally an infantry war.

At the outbreak of the Revolution the 4th Battalion of Royal Artillery were serving in America. They were destined to bear the brunt of the action for the duration of the conflict. Later four companies of the 3rd Battalion were merged into the 4th Battalion, while another four companies of the 3rd along with four of the 1st Battalion also went to America.

The regimental coat of the artillery was cut like that of the Line infantry but of blue cloth rather than red. Facings were red. Up to 1782 linings for artillery were specified as red but all pictorial evidence shows white linings. Probably another case of orders being phrased later to accommodate an item already in use by the troops. Each lapel had ten yellow metal buttons spaced equally with yellow worsted tape around the buttonholes. Cuffs had four and the collar is usually shown as having one on each side. Pockets were horizontal and it is probable that these too would be laced like those of infantry coats.

Orders of 1772 mention both whole and half-gaiters and on parade sometimes breeches with stockings only. Breeches and waistcoats were white. Shoes were black with yellow metal buckles. No doubt the artillerymen also utilised the canvas overalls like those worn by the infantry. A contemporary description of a gunner in undress lists a blue jacket and brown trousers.

Battalion Orders of 1771 state that 'Black stocks being no more a uniform part of the dress of the Battalion, the Captains or Commanding Officers of

Left to right: OFFICER OF THE ROYAL ARTILLERY
(FROCK UNIFORM).

CORPORAL OF THE ROYAL ARTILLERY IN CAMPAIGN CAP.

GUNNER OF THE 4th BATTALION, ROYAL ARTILLERY.

Left to right: TRUMPETER OF THE 17th LIGHT DRAGOONS.

OFFICER OF THE 17th LIGHT DRAGOONS.

PRIVATE OF THE 16th LIGHT DRAGOONS
(DISMOUNTED DUTY DRESS).

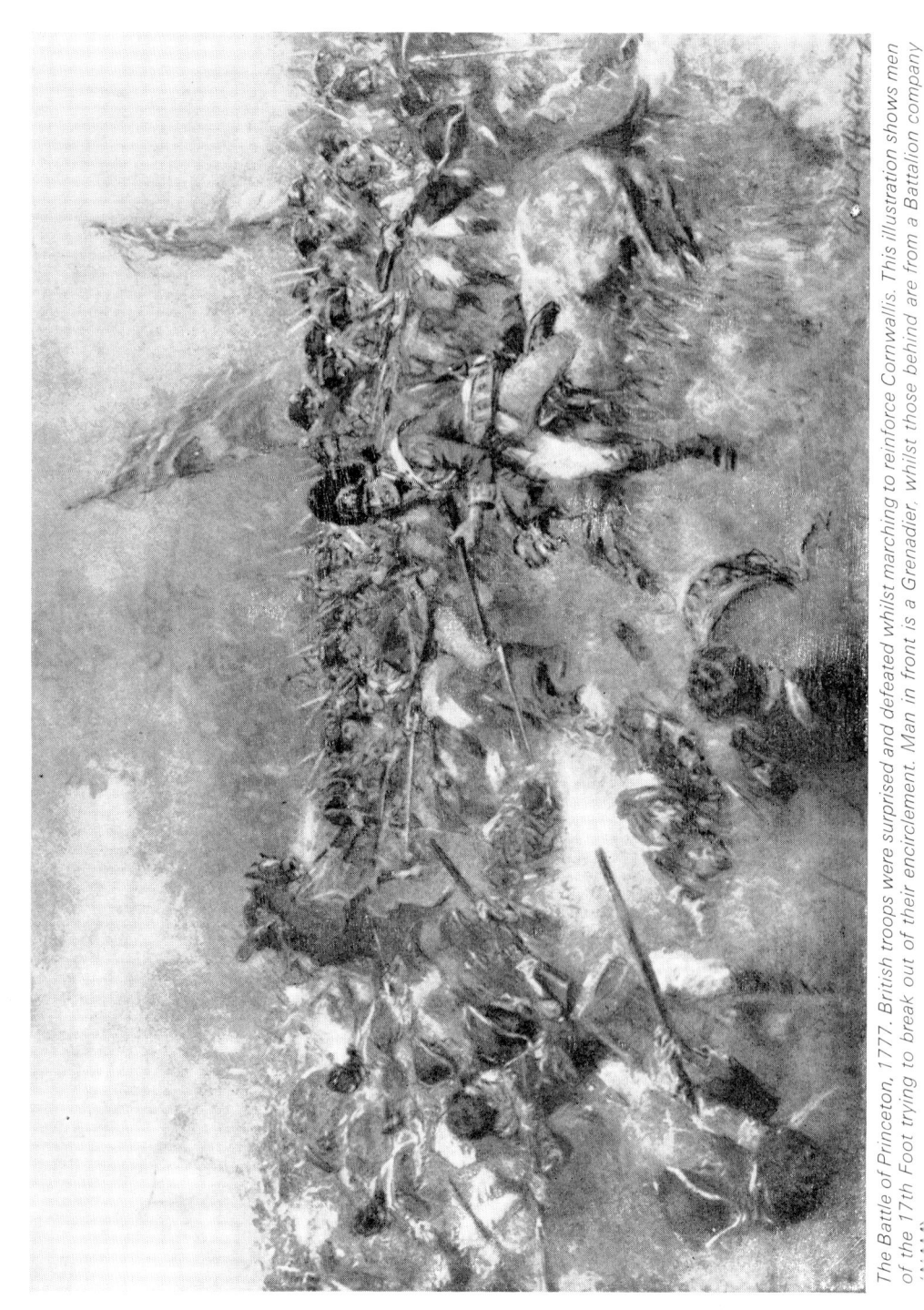

The Battle of Princeton, 1777. British troops were surprised and defeated whilst marching to reinforce Cornwallis. This illustration shows men of the 17th Foot trying to break out of their encirclement. Man in front is a Grenadier, whilst those behind are from a Battalion company

Surrender of the British Army under Cornwallis at Yorktown in 1783. Men at front are General Staff officers with, behind them men of the Battalion and Grenadier companies marching forward to surrender their arms. Also visible in the foreground is an American infantryman taking possession of some Colours, although most of the regiments were allowed to retain these according to the Laws of War (NAM).

REGIMENTAL LACE PATTERNS (MEN)

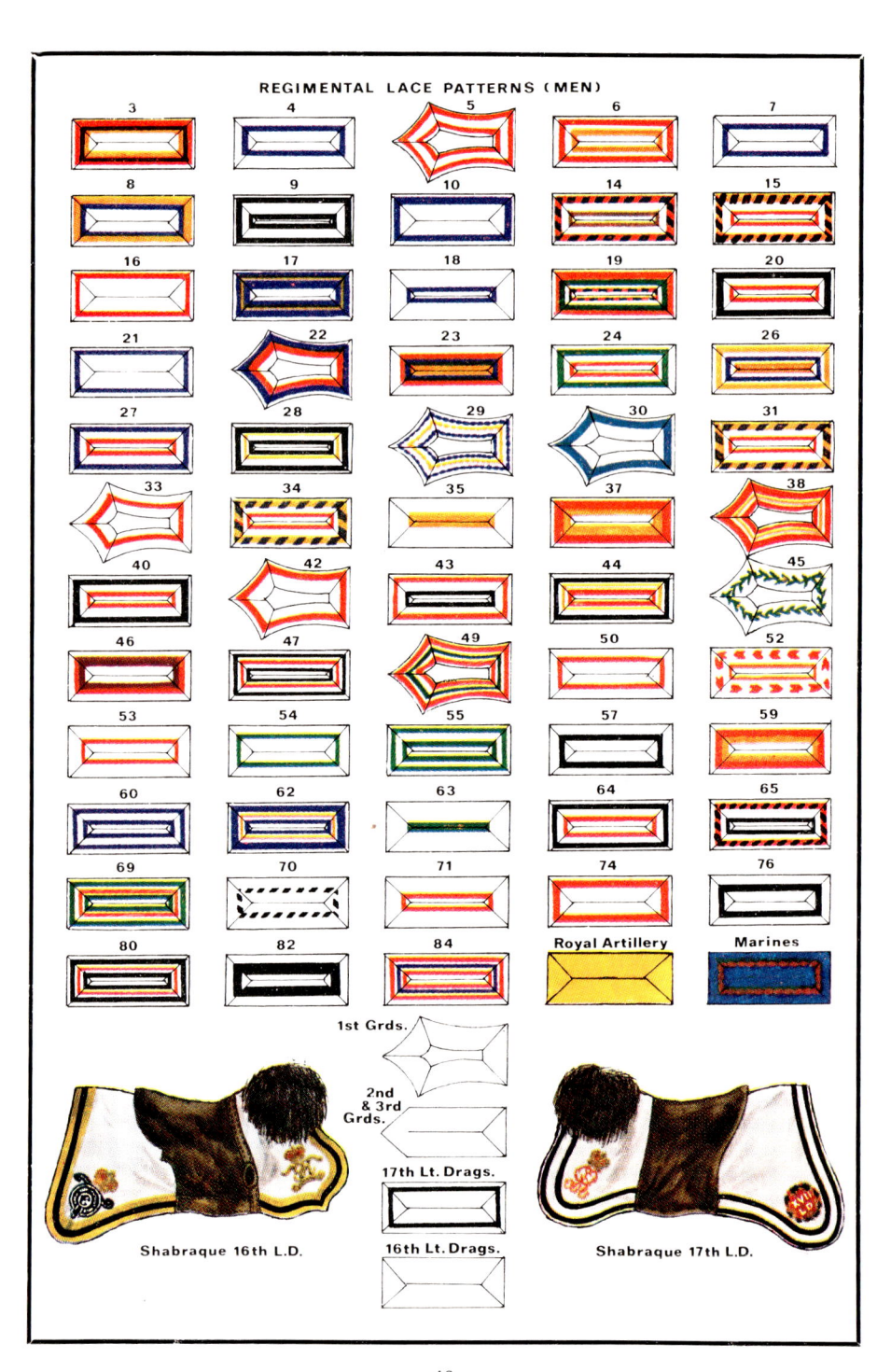

Companies are forthwith to provide the men with white ones.' Although lace for all ranks of corporal and below is specified as yellow worsted, the cocked hats are always mentioned as having 'gold lace'. A black leather cockade with a small button was worn on the hat. The 4th Battalion are recorded as wearing a black feather from the cockade. Although the cocked hat was the official headgear of the artillery, a contemporary water colour shows a gunner with Burgoyne's Army wearing a black leather cap with turned up peak, a brass comb with a red horsehair mane. Presumably the artillery found this type of cap as suitable for the American service as did the light infantry. Hair was clubbed, powdered and tied with a black bow.

Gunners carried bayonets which, like those of the infantry would be suspended from the white belt worn either over the right shoulder or around the waist. They were armed with carbines. Over the left shoulder was another white belt carrying a pouch of white leather which bore on the flap a yellow metal crown over scroll badge on a backing of red cloth. Attached all round the pouch belt was a red cord from which hung a brass mounted priming horn. On the chest of the pouch belt was a leather loop holding a hammer and prickers.

Sergeants wore gold lace around the buttonholes and on the cocked hat. Officially they carried halberds until 1845 but these were probably laid aside in the American campaign. Up to 1773 corporals wore a single gold epaulette on the right shoulder and bombardiers a single yellow worsted one. After this date corporals were given two in yellow worsted in place of one gold. After the war in 1788, corporals were ordered to wear two gold epaulettes and bombardiers one. Like the men, corporals and bombardiers carried carbines and bayonets.

ARTILLERY OFFICERS

According to various Battalion Orders of 1772, officers were clothed mainly in 'plain frocks with plain hats with a gold band and button loop'. They were to mount guard in their plain frocks, plain hats, Regimental swords (swords had replaced fusils for officers in 1770) and their hair well powdered. When the men wear whole or half-gaiters the officers do the same.'

A more ornate officer's uniform was also in use, probably for full dress. This had gold lace around the buttonholes. Full dress hats too had gold lace trim. A portrait painted after 1770 shows an officer wearing what appears to be the style of coat worn about 1760. It has a low collar and the cuffs have a four-buttoned sash edged in gold lace. The lapels have plain buttonholes but are gold laced around the edge. This could indicate that apart from the plain coats, old uniforms were worn on campaign to preserve the regimentals. Since 1770 gold epaulettes had been worn in place of the shoulder knot. Although the epaulette indicated an officer, actual ranks were not marked by this until later in the century. Also in 1770 the crimson sash which at this time was quite voluminous had been transferred from the shoulder and was now worn around the waist under the coat. As well as full or half-gaiters, officers wore boots or sometimes only stockings and buckled shoes.

In 1779 officers of the 1st and 2nd Battalions requested permission to wear the sword on the shoulder belt; this was granted. As infantry officers had been wearing belts over the right shoulder for some time before this date, it seems likely that many artillery officers followed suit before permission was even requested.

In 1782 a junior officer of artillery was equipped with the following: 1 suit

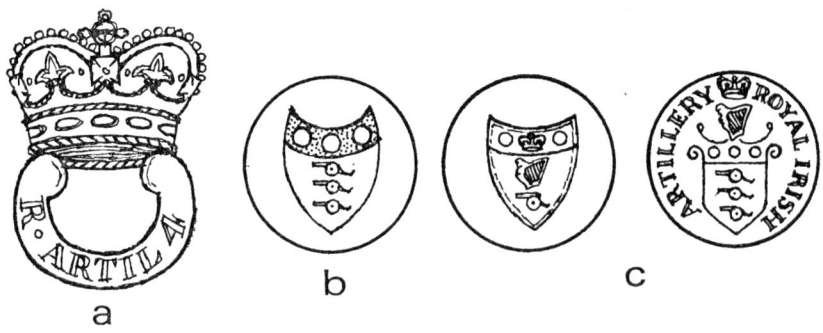

ARTILLERY DETAILS.
a. Cartridge pouch badge. Yellow metal mounted on red cloth. Pouch usually white leather.
b. Other ranks' button. Pewter (found at Fort Erie).
c. Other ranks' buttons. Royal Irish Artillery. Pewter (found at Fort George and Somerville, Massachusetts).

of full uniform, 1 frock suit of uniform, 1 laced hat, 1 plain hat, 1 regimental greatcoat, 2 pairs of boots, 3 pairs of shoes, 12 pairs of stockings, 12 shirts, 12 stocks, 6 linen waistcoats, 6 linen breeches, 12 handkerchiefs, 1 sash, 1 regimental sword, belt and clasp and 1 pair of pistols. No doubt in America were added overalls, leather caps and any other item which might suit the campaign. Mounted officers of artillery often used saddle covers of white fur or sheepskin with brown or black fur covers over the saddle holsters.

ROYAL IRISH ARTILLERY

Formed in 1755 and initially called the 'Artillery Company of Ireland', it became in 1760 'The Royal Irish Artillery'. Its first active service was in the American War. In March 1777 40 men under the command of a Royal Artillery officer embarked for America where they served throughout the war. The uniform was a blue coat faced scarlet. Cuffs and collar embroidered gold. Corporal and below wore yellow worsted lace. Cocked hat laced gold and with a black leather cockade. Breeches were white cloth and white stockings were worn with short gaiters in summer and long in winter. NCOs and men wore their hair clubbed and powdered. In 1801 the unit became part of the Royal Artillery.

ARTILLERY MUSICIANS

Like those of the infantry, drummers and fifers of artillery wore coats of reversed colours, ie red coats with blue facings and shoulder wings. They were issued with plain cocked hats but fur caps were also worn. Front flaps of the earlier cloth mitre caps bore the design of a brass mortar on a brown carriage with trophies of ramrods on either side. The front of the cap carried the Ordnance Arms, ie a shield, the lower part bearing three brass cannons on a blue ground above which were three cannon balls on a white ground. It is more than likely that a similar design decorated the metal front plates of drummers and fifers fur caps in the 1770s.

Previously coats had been laced on the seams with Royal lace and there seems no reason to suppose the practice had been discontinued. The drum shells carried a painted motif of two figures flanking a shield bearing the cannon balls and three cannons. The shield was surmounted by a decorative scroll.

For the band, two indents of 1772 give some idea of how musicians were clothed. The first, dated August 4, mentions seven coats and caps for the 'band of musick' and one of each for the Music-Major. The second, dated August 26, is for the production of 'eight plain scarlet frocks with blue lapels . . . and likewise a Frock and White Waistcoat and Breeches of Serjeant's cloth for the 1st Musician with a pattern of two cheap epaulettes of blue cloth between small laces and a slight gold fringe for the last mentioned suit . . . nine plain hats for the band one of which is to be a serjeants with Gold Twist loop for the First Musician.' No mention is made of swords or belts until 1789, well after the termination of the war.

4: Cavalry Uniforms

AS has already been stated, the American War was basically an infantry conflict with the terrain being as unsuitable for horsed troops as it was for artillery. In the American theatre of operations the main functions of the cavalry soldier were patrol and scouting duties, although a few mounted actions such as Pound Ridge in July 1779 were fought.

On many occasions the shortage of horses made it necessary for cavalrymen to serve as foot soldiers.

Only two British cavalry regiments took part in the war. They were the 16th The Queen's Light Dragoons and the 17th Light Dragoons.

It was the 17th that saw action first. Leaving Ireland in 1775 they arrived in Boston just in time for a detachment to join the reinforcements for Bunker Hill. The regiment had recently been brought up to strength with heavy drafts from other units before departure.

In July 1776 the 16th Light Dragoons arrived in America. The regiment was engaged at Paoli, Brandywine and Monmouth before transferring its effective men and mounts to the 17th Light Dragoons and returning to England. The combined regiments were popularly known as the 'Queen's Dragoons'. As such this unit operated throughout the war from its headquarters on Long Island, being principally engaged around New York.

A detachment served with the Loyalist Legion of Banastre Tarleton in the Southern campaign and was interned after Yorktown. As uniforms were difficult to replace in the field, it seems unlikely that the transferred men of the 16th would wear anything but their own red coats faced blue. Further, the blue facings were the mark of a Royal regiment and one feels that few would wish to exchange them for the white facings of the 17th Light Dragoons. The cavalry returned to England in 1783.

THE 16th LIGHT DRAGOONS

Coats were scarlet faced dark blue (collar, cuffs and lapels) and lined white. Each lapel had ten pewter buttons set in pairs, the buttonholes bound in white lace. Each sleeve, just above the cuff, and each rear skirt of the coat had four buttons set in pairs, each button placed at the centre of a chevron of white lace. Two pieces of lace were set on each side of the rear centre vent, the top pair having buttons on the outer ends. The collar had a button and lace on each side and was cut to a point at the back. On each shoulder was a white tufted worsted epaulette. By the 1768 Clothing Warrant these epaulettes should have been of the facing colour edged with white tape but all-white seemed to have been more common.

Waistcoats and breeches were white, the former having a flapped horizontal pocket at each side. Stocks were black except for Sundays and parades when white stocks were worn. Black boots covered the knee in front but were stepped down at the sides and around the back to enable the knee to be bent. Spurs were steel. The men wore brown or black cloth gaiters for dismounted duties.

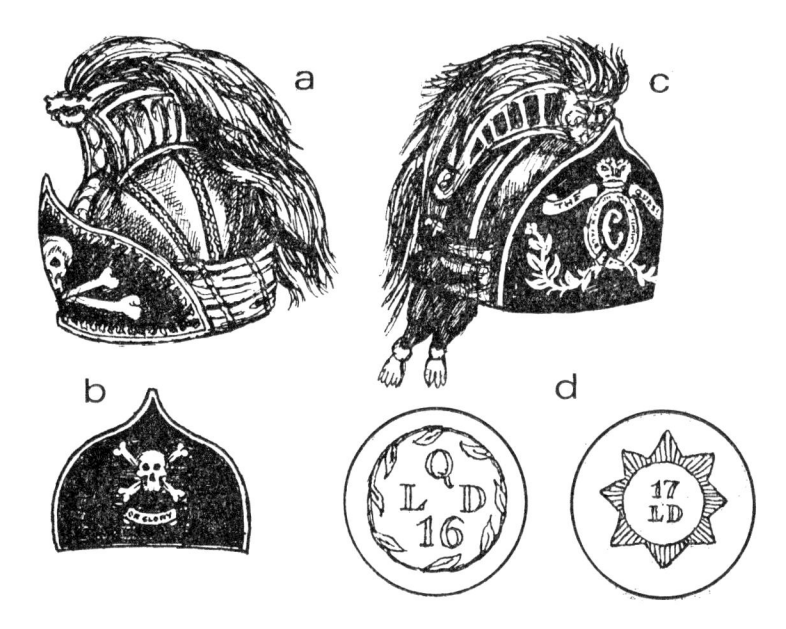

CAVALRY DETAILS.
a. Officer's helmet. 17th Light Dragoons. 1780.
b. Alternative cap plate design for 17th Light Dragoons.
c. Helmet of 16th Light Dragoons. 1780.
d. Officer's silver buttons. 16th and 17th Light Dragoons.
(Trooper's buttons were same design in pewter. 17th had larger star on men's buttons.)

A white leather belt over the left shoulder carried a black leather cartridge pouch buckled at the back and a carbine swivel. The sword was carried either on a belt over the right shoulder or in a frog on a white waistbelt. Although a waistbelt was only official for dragoons and dragoon guards, contemporary sources show this method worn by light dragoons with the belt having a small black leather 'belly-box' ammunition pouch on the front. The sword was a single stirrup hilted weapon with a straight blade carried in a black leather scabbard with steel mounts. Bayonets were also carried.

The head-dress of the 16th was the regimental pattern of the current light dragoon helmet. It consisted of a black leather cap reinforced up the sides with white metal strips. Across the top, from front to rear, was a black japanned metal crest with white metal fittings. To this was fitted a red horsehair mane. A vertical front plate of black japanned metal was edged with white metal and carried the regimental motif embossed in white metal. In the centre of the badge was the letter 'C' (for Queen Charlotte). Surrounding this was the garter with the motto (Honi soit qui mal y pense) and above a crown flanked by two scrolls bearing the words 'THE QUEEN'S'.

Around the lower edges of the garter was a laurel leaf pattern. One illustration of the helmet shows a scroll along the bottom of the garter possibly bearing the regiment's motto 'Aut cursu, aut conimus armis'. Around the bottom of the helmet (behind the front plate) was a black silk turban with white tassels at the back. Watering caps of red cloth with a turn-up flap in the facing colour were also worn. On the flap was the regimental device. Hair was worn unpowdered except on Sundays and parades.

The saddle housings were white with an edge of Royal lace (yellow with a blue centre stripe). The front and rear portions of the housings were joined by a tan leather seat which fitted the saddle.

The rear of the housings carried the garter badge in blue with blue scrolls above and a yellow crown (red cushions). The front bore the Royal cypher (GR) in yellow with blue scrolls, edged yellow, above and below, with the regiment's title and number. The crown surmounting these was coloured like that on the rear. The saddle holsters were covered with white fur. A white curcingle around the leather seat fastened the housings to the saddle. Cloaks were red with blue collar and lining. These were carried rolled behind the saddle. The cloaks had fastening clasps at the throat set on strips of Royal lace.

Besides six mounted troops (when horses were available) a dismounted troop was added to the Regiment in 1776. Instead of a cloak these men had a loose mantle which was fastened over the knapsack. They wore brown cloth gaiters in place of boots and did not carry swords. They were equipped with hatchets or bill-hooks and acted independently as light infantry.

Sergeants had narrow silver lace around the buttonholes, collar and the edge of the blue epaulette (fringed silver). Sergeants' waist sashes were crimson spun silk with a blue centre stripe, tied on the right.

Corporals had a narrow silver lace around the top edge of the cuffs and a white silk tape edge and fringe on the epaulettes.

OFFICERS

Officers were dressed in a manner similar to the men but with the usual refinements of fabric. Lace was silver and epaulettes were either of blue velvet with silver lace decorations or all silver. Designs varied but they were either fringed or tasselled silver. When the sword was carried on a shoulder belt the belt was white leather and was worn over the right shoulder under the coat. It had a silver oval belt plate on which was engraved the badge and title of the Regiment. The waist sash of crimson silk was knotted on the right side as opposed to the infantry who tied theirs on the left.

The regulation boots with high tops were often replaced by a pair of jockey or hunting style boots with tan cuffs around the tops and reaching to below the knee.

Swords were stirrup hilted like those of the men but of finer quality. Sword knots were white leather.

The helmets were also similar but of better quality than the men's. They had the front plate and comb decoration in silver rather than embossed white metal.

Officers' saddle housings were white edged in gold lace with a blue centre stripe. The embroidery followed that of the men's with gold replacing yellow thread.

FARRIERS

Farriers wore blue coats with only the collar and cuffs in red. Lapels and linings were blue, lace was white. Waistcoats and breeches were also blue. Instead of a helmet the farrier wore a small bearskin cap with a red cloth patch behind. At the front was a black japanned plate with a horseshoe design embossed in white metal. A white belt over the right shoulder carried an axe at the left hip. When the troop was mounted with drawn swords, the farrier carried this axe, blade uppermost with the edge turned in towards the horses head, the shaft on the thigh. This was called 'Axe Advanced'.

On parades they wore white leather aprons under their coats which were rolled back at the left side.

The saddle housings were similar to the mens but often bore badges of crossed hammers, pincers and horseshoes. The fur covers on the front of the saddle were black. They covered not holsters but 'churns', ie cylindrical leather buckets which carried horseshoes and farrier's tools. A cape was carried behind the saddle.

TRUMPETERS

According to the Royal Warrant of 1768 the 16th Light Dragoons were not one of those regiments whose musicians wore coats of reversed colours. They wore red coats faced with blue and laced with Royal lace. The lace would in all probability have been sewn around seams and the edge of facings and possibly in chevrons or half hoops up the sleeves. Laced wings were also often worn by trumpeters. Waistcoats, breeches and coat linings were white.

The Warrant also directed that trumpeters of light dragoons should wear cocked hats with a plume in the facing colour of the regiment. However, it was often the practice for trumpeters to wear helmets like the troop. Trumpeters' swords were usually brass hilted with scimitar blades. Scabbards were of black leather with metal fittings. Brass trumpets were carried on a cord over the left shoulder. The cords were interwoven red and blue with a metallic thread through. As well as the trumpet some trumpeters carried bugle horns. These were something like the hoop shape of a French horn and were carried looped over the shoulder with the arm through the hoop. It was used as a signal to assemble the troop.

Saddle housings for trumpeters followed those of the men.

THE 17th LIGHT DRAGOONS

The coats of the 17th Light Dragoons were much the same as those of the 16th but with collar, cuffs and lapels faced white. The buttonhole lace was white with a black line at the edge. The pewter buttons were set in pairs and were marked 17 L.D. Coat linings, waistcoats and breeches were white. The men's coats had two epaulettes of white worsted with a tufted fringe. Black stocks were worn (white on Sundays and parades).

Black boots with tinned spurs were worn (with white linen knee protectors over the breeches). On dismounted duties, short cloth gaiters were worn. Pouch and sword belts were of white leather and were usually worn over the shoulders although occasionally a waistbelt with sword and black leather 'belly-box' is shown in contemporary pictures. The sword was carried in a black leather scabbard with brass fittings. The sword knot was white leather. Carbines and bayonets were also carried.

The helmet of the 17th consisted of a brass skull and decorative comb which held a red horsehair mane. The metal front plate was japanned black with a white edge and bore the regiment's badge of a skull and crossbones in white embossed metal. The actual design of the badge appears to have had a number of variations. The most usual pattern has the bones crossed behind the skull with a scroll below inscribed 'OR GLORY'. The variations include the bones crossed above the skull with the scroll above this and the skull with bones crossed below without any scroll. There is also evidence that the badge was sometimes painted on in white rather than embossed. The helmet turban was red with white tassels on the ends. It was held in place with fine white metal chains. According to the 1768 Warrant the turban should have been in the facing colour ie white but all contemporary evidence shows red or crimson.

The detachment of the 17th which served in the Southern Campaign with Tarleton refused to adopt the Loyalist green coats of his Legion. They preferred to wear their own patched and repaired red coats. During hot weather this detachment wore white linen frocks (also for stable duty). They also replaced their red helmet turbans with bands of white sheepskin.

The saddle cloth was white edged in white lace with black edges. The front portion bore the Royal cypher above the regimental number both in red embroidery. The GR was surmounted by a yellow crown with red cushions. On the rear corner of the back portion was a patch of red cloth with the numbers 'XVII' over 'L.D.' in white.

This was surrounded by a wreath of flowers and leaves in natural colours. The saddle holster covers were of black fur. The front and rear portions were joined by a tan seat over the saddle. The cloak was red lined white with a white collar. It was fastened at the throat by metal clasps set on strips of regimental lace. When carried behind the saddle the cloak was rolled to show the white lining at the ends.

Rank distinctions for NCOs would be similar to those specified for the 16th Light Dragoons.

OFFICERS

Officers wore similar coats to the men with the usual refinements. Lace was silver with a black line around the edge. Buttons were silver marked 17 L.D. inside a star and epaulettes were either silver lace or silver lace worked on a white cloth ground. Both would have a silver fringe. The regulation waistcoat was white with two horizontal pockets and a single row of small silver regimental buttons (sometimes a closely set double row is shown in contemporary pictures). Breeches were white and silver spurs were worn with the high regulation boots. Often non-regulation boots were worn.

Black stocks were usual on field service but scarlet velvet ones were worn for parades. An inspection return for the period gives white helmet turbans for officers and dark blue cloaks lined white. White gloves were worn for parades.

A portrait by Joshua Reynolds of an officer of the regiment in 1769 shows a crimson shoulder belt with silver edges. More usually, however, the belt was white leather with a silver belt plate. It was worn either under or over the coat.

An inspection report as early as 1771 describes the belt plate as silver with the King's cypher embossed in gold and black. The sword had a single strirup hilt of gilt with a white leather knot. It was carried in a black leather scabbard mounted with gilt fittings. The waist sash of crimson silk was tied on the right side.

Officers' helmets were similar to those of the men with silver fittings in place of white metal and of better quality. The turban (despite the 'inspection' return) is usually shown as crimson silk held with silver chains.

Horse furniture for officers followed the pattern of the men's but with gold and silver embroidery in place of yellow and white. Farriers were dressed like those of the 16th but with the appropriate regimental differences in facings and badges.

TRUMPETERS

Trumpeters of the 17th Light Dragoons wore white coats with red collar, cuffs, lapels and linings. The buttonholes were laced with regimental lace (ie white with a black edge). The seams and sleeves were also laced (the sleeves with chevrons). The coats had red shoulder wings barred and edged with lace. Buttons were pewter set in twos. Waistcoats and breeches were red, and black boots were worn with white knee protectors inside. Spurs were tinned.

Swords for trumpeters were scimitar-bladed with brass hilts. They were carried in black leather scabbards on a white waistbelt.

Although laced cocked hats with white plumes were worn by the regiments' trumpeters, it is known that they also wore helmets like the men. The cocked hats are more likely to have been worn on dress parades. Saddle housings were like those of the men but with white fur holster covers in place of black. The cloak was carried behind the saddle.

Trumpets were brass with cords of red and white intertwined. The antique bugle horns described for the 16th were also carried by some trumpeters of the 17th.

NOTES COMMON TO BOTH REGIMENTS

Reins and bridles for officers and men of light dragoon regiments were of black leather. The horses' steel bits were usually straight. Stirrups were round.

The following note on equipment is taken from a publication of 1778 by Hinde:

'The equipment for the regiments sent to America included four rifled carbines per troop, corn sacks, nose bags with leather bottoms and straps, forage cords, havre sacks with leather straps, water bottles, pickets, 60 scythes with stones, water decks, hair breast lines for pickets, felling axes, great mallets, water buckets, iron kettles with bags, water canteens with leather straps, hand hatchets, bell tents, camp colours and 192 bill hooks for the dismounted men.'

5: Colours

A DETAILED explanation of the designs and issue of Regimental Colours is too complex a subject to fall within the scope of this book. Designs of Colours of the Foot Guards, for instance, followed a complicated pattern with each company carrying a different emblem. The following is a general guide to the Colours of Line regiments with certain known facts relevant to the American War.

Colours carried by the British Army during the American Revolution were those of the pattern specified in the Warrant of 1768. It is now impossible to be categorical about the design of the Colours of each regiment as many were destroyed during the campaign. Further, the centre decoration which contained a regiment's title varied considerably in individual interpretation. Some regiments used a neat wreath of flowers while others employed the more fashionable flamboyant spray. Others carried the Garter badge in place of the floral wreath.

Following the Warrant of 1768, Infantry Colours were to be 6 feet 6 inches on the fly by 6 feet in depth. The length of the staff was 9 feet 10 inches from the tip of the spearhead to the foot. Cords and tassels were interwoven crimson and gold.

The First Colour (King's Colour) of a regiment was the Union Flag (at this period the red diagonal cross of Ireland had not been added). In the centre was painted or embroidered in gold Roman numerals, the number and rank of the regiment together with the abbreviation REGT. This was surrounded by a wreath of roses and thistles in natural colours on a common stalk (or if not, a blue garter with gold inscription).

Regiments allowed to wear a special badge (see Appendix A for details) used it in the centre of the King's colour and marked the number of the regiment in the first canton of the flag (nearest the staff).

The Second or Regimental Colour was in the facing colour of the regiment with the Union in the first canton. Regiments with red or white facings carried a red St George's Cross on a white ground. Those regiments with black facings had a red St George's Cross on a black ground. The same centre decorations as in the King's Colour was painted or embroidered on (also with the regimental number on the Union in the first canton). Regiments with special badges also had devices in the three other corners of their Regimental Colour (see Appendix A for details).

Although Colours were carried in the field during the earlier engagements of the war, the practice became less frequent as the conflict progressed. Many sets of Colours were captured and many destroyed. The fate of some of those lost is known and is as follows:

Two sets of Colours of the 7th Fusiliers were captured. One at Fort Chamble in 1775 and the other at Cowpens in 1779.

The Colours of the 43rd, 76th and 80th Regiments were taken after the surrender at Yorktown.

COLOURS.
a. Centre design of Regimental Colour. 9th Foot.

b. Regimental Colour. 33rd Foot.

c. King's Colour. 9th Foot.

d. Centre design of King's Colour. 7th Foot (Royal Fusiliers).
Colour schemes follow those described in text.

The 17th Foot lost its Colours at Stony Point in 1779 and had none to surrender at Yorktown.

The 33rd Foot surrendered at Yorktown but its Colours eventually came home and were deposited in Taunton in 1787.

Some Colours were concealed and smuggled out of America. Although the 9th Foot surrendered at Saratoga, the Colours were hidden and taken to England by Colonel Hill.

Similarly after Yorktown the Colours of the 23rd Fusiliers were saved due to a Captain Peter and another officer wrapping them around their bodies and concealing them in their baggage later.

One set of Colours was lost even before the regiment reached America. The 81st Foot were in 1778 sailing from England to Ireland *en route* for the war when their vessel was set on by American privateers and their Colours captured. The Regiment did not serve in the war.

CAVALRY GUIDONS

Following the Warrant of 1768, the guidons of the 16th and 17th Light Dragoons would probably be of the swallow-tailed variety. They were to be of silk with the design more probably painted on than embroidered. The cords and tassels were of crimson silk and gold mixed.

The number of guidons per regiment depended on the number of troops making up the regiment. It worked out roughly at two guidons for every six troops. Some regiments with nine troops carried three guidons.

The guidon set consisted of the King's or First Guidon and the Regimental or Second Guidon.

Where a regiment had three guidons, the third bore a figure 3 on a circular patch of red below the centre scroll.

It is unlikely that either the 16th or the 17th Light Dragoons carried their guidons in the actions fought in America. First, there was little opportunity for cavalry actions on the European style which facilitated the guidons being displayed. Secondly, the role of the light dragoons was so often as foot soldiers that the carrying of guidons would have been impractical.

Appendix A: Notes on each Regiment in America

The following list gives the regiments which served in America together with their facing colours, style of lace and other remarks. The figure 2 behind the style of lace indicates that laces were set in pairs for other ranks. Officers often wore paired lace even in regiments where the men's lace was spaced singly. Also officers often dispensed with lace altogether.

In general, yellow facings appear to have been nearer yellow ochre in colour, greens a dull olive or dull blue green and buffs almost cream (regiments with buff facings also had buff waistcoats, breeches linings and belts). Any variations in basic colours have been noted in brackets following the facing colour. Style of lace is indicated by the word square or bastion (spearpoint loop). Officers of regiments which had bastion lace for the men usually wore gold or silver square-ended lace themselves. The regimental lace patterns worn by other ranks are shown in a colour plate.

Key

(F) Facing Colour, (L) Style of Lace, (O) Colour of Officers' Lace. The titles in brackets following the number of a regiment is the later designation. These were not used at the time of the American War.

Foot Regiments
3rd The Buffs (Royal East Kent Regiment)
(F) Buff, (L) Square 2, (O) Silver.
Described as a very young battalion. Arrived in June 1781 and had one campaign in the Carolinas (was at Eutaw Springs in September 1781) went to West Indies in December 1782
Dragon badge on Colours, drums and grenadier caps.

4th King's Own (King's Own Royal Regiment (Lancaster))
(F) Blue, (L) Square, (O) Silver.
Were in America at outbreak of war (since 1774). Fought at Lexington, Bunker Hill, New York, Germantown. Went to Florida in November 1778 then on to West Indies. King's cypher badge on Colours, drums and grenadier caps. Officers' belt plate (1774) Gilt, rectangular, lion over IV. Other ranks: Brass plate with milled edge, lion over IV within oval crowned garter. Portrait of an officer of 1780 shows silver buttons marked IVth but button found in America bears Arabic 4. In 1769 officers were recorded as having no lace, only silver embroidered buttonholes.

5th (Royal Northumberland Fusiliers)
(F) Gosling Green (dull yellowish green), (L) Bastion, (O) Silver.
In America at outbreak of war (since 1774). Fought at Lexington, Bunker Hill, Brooklyn, Brandywine, Germantown. Went to Florida in November 1778 then on to West Indies. The badge of St George on Colours, drums and grenadier and battalion fur caps and light company helmets.

Although not classified as fusiliers till after the war, the entire Regiment except the light company wore bearskin caps. Battalion company men wore slightly smaller caps to the grenadiers and without the grenade badge on the rear. They did not carry match cases or swords like the grenadiers. Report of 1769 states officers' coats not laced. Regiment wore heavy brown cloth gaiters on service in place of half spatterdashes. High black gaiters on parade.

6th (Royal Warwickshire Regiment)
(F) Deep Yellow (Raw Sienna), (L) Square, (O) Silver.

Detachments arrived in New York in October 1776 but were of insufficient strength and were sent home the same year. One detachment was with Ferguson as riflemen at Brandywine in September 1777. Antelope badge was worn on Colours, drums and grenadier caps.

7th Royal Fusiliers (City of London Regiment)
(F) Blue, (L) Square, (O) Gold.

Were in Quebec in 1773, served here and in New York. Returned to British Isles in 1783. Badge of Rose in Garter on Colours, drums and grenadier and battalion fur caps. As this was a fusilier regiment the battalion companies wore the bearskin cap. It was slightly smaller than that of the grenadiers without the grenade at the rear. Battalion companies did not carry match cases or swords like the grenadiers.

8th The King's (King's (Liverpool) Regiment)
(F) Blue, (L) Square, (O) Gold.

Arrived in Quebec in 1768. Fought at Fort Stanwix and saw service on the Great Lakes. Remained in Canada until September 1785 when they returned to British Isles. Badge of White Horse on Colours, drums and grenadier caps.

9th (Royal Norfolk Regiment)
(F) Bright Yellow, (L) Square, (O) Silver.

Arrived in Quebec in May 1776. Served with Burgoyne's army in campaign of 1777. Surrendered at Saratoga. Interned until return to British Isles in 1781.

10th (Royal Lincolnshire Regiment)
(F) Bright Yellow, (L) Square, (O) Silver.

Were in Boston at outbreak of war. Fought at Lexington, Bunker Hill, Brooklyn, Bronx (NY) Brandywine. Returned home in December 1778.

14th (West Yorkshire Regiment (Prince of Wales' Own)
(F) Pale Buff, (L) Square, (O) Silver.

Were in Boston in 1768. Detachment served at Brandywine as riflemen for Ferguson's Loyalists. Fought at Great Bridge, Virginia in 1775. Returned to British Isles in summer of 1777. Caps for drummers were white bearskin.

15th (East Yorkshire Regiment (Duke of York's Own))
(F) Philamort Yellow (Yellow Ochre), (L) Square, (O) Silver.

Arrived in America in May 1776. Served in New York campaigns of 1776 at Brandywine Germantown, Rhode Island, Charleston. Went to Florida in November 1778 then on to West Indies.

16th (Bedfordshire and Hertfordshire Regiment)
(F) Philamort Yellow, (L) Square, (O) Silver.

Detachment arrived in New York in August 1776. Fought in the Georgia campaign of 1779. Detachments at Baton Rouge 1779 and Pensacola 1781. Returned to British Isles in 1782.

17th (Royal Leicestershire Regiment)
(F) White (Greyish), (L) Square, (O) Silver.

Arrived in Boston in December 1775. Fought in New York and New Jersey campaigns of 1776-77 and at Brandywine, Germantown, Monmouth. Captured twice, Stony Point in 1779 (exchanged) and Yorktown 1781. Interned until 1783 then exchanged again. Inspection Report of June 1775 lists silver gorgets, numbered buttons and laced epaulette for officers but makes no mention of buttonhole lace. Swords silver hilted with gold and crimson knots. Light company caps had 'large round peaks, straight up in front'. Colours received in 1766 were lost at Stony Point in 1779. When the Regiment returned home a new set was presented in 1787, a somewhat unusual occurrence.

18th Royal Irish (Royal Irish Regiment)
(F) Blue, (L) Square, (O) Gold.

Arrived in Boston in 1774. Fought at Lexington, Bunker Hill. Moved to Nova Scotia then returned to British Isles in July 1776. Harp badge on Colours, drums and grenadier caps.

19th (Green Howards, Alexandra, Princess of Wales' Own Yorkshire Regiment)
(F) Deep Green (Dark Brownish Green), (L) Square, (O) Gold.

Arrived Charleston, South Carolina in June 1781. Present at Monks Corner, Relief of Fort Ninety-Six and Eutaw Springs. Left for West Indies in December 1782. Inspection Report of May 1775 states that officers' coats had no lace or embroidery, buttons numbered and with epaulettes. Light company officers had white instead of red waistcoats. In 1777 it was noted that 'hats and light company caps not according to regulations'.

20th (Lancashire Fusiliers)
(F) Pale Yellow), (L) Square 2, (O) Silver.

Arrived in Quebec in May 1776. Served with Burgoyne through campaigns of 1777 until surrender at Saratoga. Interned until return to British Isles in 1781. According to Inspection Reports of 1769 and 1775 the regiment was well equipped. Officers' coats had laced buttonholes and numbered buttons. The sword belts are noted as being worn over the shoulder at this time. In 1775 a 'good band of eight musicians existed'.

21st Royal North British Fusiliers (Royal Scots Fusiliers)
(F) Blue, (L) Square, (O) Gold.

Arrived in Quebec in May 1776. Served here and on Lake Champlain then with Burgoyne in campaign of 1777. Interned after Saratoga until returned to British Isles in 1781. Thistle badge on Colours, drums and grenadier and battalion fur caps. As a fusilier regiment the battalion companies wore the bearskin caps. Slightly smaller than those of the grenadiers and without the grenade on the rear. Battalion companies did not carry swords or match cases as did the grenadiers.

22nd (Cheshire Regiment)
(F) Pale Buff, (L) Bastion 2, (O) Gold.

Arrived in Boston in July 1775. Fought in New York and New Jersey campaigns of 1776 being garrisoned here for the greater part of the war.
   Returned to British Isles in 1783. Inspection Report of 1769 shows officers had gorgets and buff epaulettes laced with gold.

23rd Royal Welch Fusiliers
(F) Blue, (L) Square, (O) Gold.

Arrived in New York in June 1773. Fought at Lexington and Bunker Hill (at this engagement out of a grenadier company of 3 officers and 70 men, only 5 came through unscathed). Served as Marines with Howe's fleet for some time. Then under Clinton and Cornwallis fighting at New York, Brandywine and Camden. Surrendered at Yorktown in 1781, interned until peace, then returned to British Isles in 1783. Badge of Prince of Wales' feathers on Colours, drums and grenadier and battalion fur caps. As a fusilier regiment the battalion companies wore bearskin caps slightly smaller than those of the grenadiers and without the grenade at rear. Battalion companies had no match cases or swords like the grenadiers. Report of 1771 states that light company wore black leather caps with red turned up front peak and black silk turban. The cap was surmounted by a black fur crest and white side plume on the left. There is a note of a review in the American War in which 'the Royal Regiment of Welch Fusiliers were preceded by a Goat with gilded horns and adorned with ringlets of flowers'.

24th (South Wales Borderers)
(F) Willow Green (Dark Bluish Green), (L) Square, (O) Silver.

Arrived in Quebec in May 1776. Served with Burgoyne's army surrendering at Saratoga in 1777. Interned until end of war.

26th Cameronians (Scottish Rifles)
(F) Pale Yellow, (L) Square, (O) Silver.

Were in Quebec in 1767, went to New York in May 1776. Fought in New Jersey campaign of 1777 and at Forts Montgomery and Clinton in October 1777, then at Monmouth in 1778. Returned to British Isles in 1780.

27th Inniskilling Regiment (Royal Inniskilling Fusiliers)
(F) Pale Buff, (L) Square 2, (O) Gold.

Arrived in Boston October 1775. Joined Howe's forces and fought in New York and at Brandywine. Went to West Indies in 1778. Castle badge on Colours, drums and grenadiers caps.

28th (Gloucestershire Regiment)
(F) Bright Yellow, (L) Square, (O) Silver.

Arrived with Cornwallis, Cape Fear, May 1776. In New York campaign of 1776, Brandywine Germantown. Went to West Indies in 1778.

29th (Worcestershire Regiment)
(F) Bright Yellow, (L) Bastion, (O) Silver.
Were in Boston in 1768. Took part in relief of Quebec in May 1776. Some companies served as additional gunners on vessels *Thunderer, Inflexible* and *Carleton* in actions on Lake Champlain. Grenadier and light companies with Burgoyne at Hubbardton and Saratoga. Headquarters and battalion companies engaged in Canada during the war. Returned to British Isles in 1787. Inspection report of 1774 noted ten Negro drummers in Regiment and buttons on grenadiers gaiters white metal. Officers are noted as not wearing buttonhole lace in America.

30th (East Lancashire Regiment)
(F) Pale Yellow, (L) Bastion, (O) Silver.
Arrived with reinforcements in 1781. Had one campaign in the Carolinas then accompanied Carolina Loyalists to Jamaica in December 1782.

31st (East Surrey Regiment)
(F) Buff, (L) Square, (O) Silver.
Arrived in Quebec in May 1776 and garrisoned City during war. Grenadier and light companies served with Burgoyne's army. Interned after Saratoga. Released in 1781.

33rd (Duke of Wellington's Regiment (West Riding))
(F) Red, (L) Bastion, (O) Silver.
Arrived with Cornwallis at Cape Fear in May 1776. Served throughout the entire war. At Long Island, New York, Charleston and campaigns in Virginia and the Carolinas. Surrendered at Yorktown in 1781. Interned until the peace. Inspection report of July 1775 gives officers' coats as scarlet faced scarlet with silver epaulettes, lace and numbered buttons. Silver laced hats. Silver mounted swords with gold and crimson knots. In 1775 the men's lace was ordered to be altered from square to bastion. Battalion men's coats had two shoulder straps rather than the usual one.

34th (The Border Regiment)
(F) Bright Yellow, (L) Square 2, (O) Silver.
Arrived in Quebec in May 1776. Saw hard service in the backwoods. Grenadier and light companies with Burgoyne until surrender at Saratoga. Released in 1781. Returned to British Isles from Canada in 1786. Inspection report of July 1775 mentions numbered buttons and silver laced hats for officers.

35th (Royal Sussex Regiment)
(F) Orange (Brownish Yellow), (L) Square, (O) Silver.
Arrived in Boston in 1775. Grenadier and light companies at Bunker Hill. Regiment in New York campaign of 1776. Stationed in this area for greater part of war. Went to West Indies in 1778.

37th (Royal Hampshire Regiment)
(F) Bright Yellow, (L) Square, (O) Silver.
Arrived with Cornwallis at Cape Fear, May 1776. Served throughout entire war, New York, Brandywine, Germantown, Monmouth, Charleston. In New York during latter part of war. Left in 1783. It was noted that drummers and fifers were trained to play both instruments.

38th (South Staffordshire Regiment)
(F) Bright Yellow, (L) Bastion, (O) Silver.
Arrived in Boston in 1774. At Lexington, Bunker Hill then New York campaign of 1776. Served here greater part of the war. Left New York in 1783 going to Nova Scotia for several years. Inspection Report of 1769 states that officers had silver embroidered buttonholes, epaulettes, numbered buttons and silver laced hats.

40th (South Lancashire Regiment (Prince of Wales' Volunteers))
(F) Buff, (L) Square, (O) Gold.
Arrived in Boston, June 1775. In New York and New Jersey campaigns of 1776–77, Brandywine, Germantown, Monmouth. Went to Florida in November 1778 then on to West Indies. Grenadiers are said to have worn white fur caps. Inspection Report of June 1769 lists officers' coats as being without lace but with gold epaulettes and gold laced hats. In 1772 the officers of the light company are noted as having no lace and white waistcoats in place of red.

42nd Royal Highland Regiment (Black Watch)
(F) Blue, (L) Bastion, (O) Gold.
Arrived in New York, July 1776. Fought at Long Island, New York and New Jersey campaigns of 1776–77, Charleston, Brandywine, Monmouth. The regiment particularly distinguished itself at the storming of Fort Washington in November 1776. Went to Florida in 1778. Returned to New York then on to Nova Scotia in 1783. Returned to British Isles in 1787. St Andrew's Badge on Colours, drums and grenadier caps. Inspection Reports (June 1769 and 1775) give officers'

coats as being laced gold with numbered buttons. Belts were of black leather. Shoulder belts were received in 1772. Grenadiers declined to wear broadswords. Orderly book of 1781 describes sergeants' kilts as being blue, black, green and scarlet stripes. Also red and yellow stripes added to the tartans for drummers.

43rd (Oxfordshire and Buckinghamshire Light Infantry)
(F) White, (L) Square, (O) Silver.
Arrived in Boston, July 1774. Fought at Lexington (flank companies), Bunker Hill, New York. Under Howe, Clinton and Cornwallis the regiment served in New Jersey, Virginia and the Carolinas (1776–81), Surrendered at Yorktown 1781. Returned to British Isles in 1783.

44th (Essex Regiment)
(F) Bright Yellow, (L) Square, (O) Silver.
Arrived in Boston in June 1775. In New York and New Jersey campaigns of 1776–77, Brandywine, Germantown. Went to Canada in 1780. Returned to British Isles in 1786.

45th (Sherwood Foresters (Nottinghamshire and Derbyshire Regiment))
(F) Deep Green (Dark Bluish Green), (L) Bastion, (O) Silver.
Arrived in Boston in July 1775. In New York campaign of 1776. Flank companies were at Brandywine and Germantown. Returned to British Isles in December 1778 with only 100 men. Inspection Report of May 1769 states officers had embroidered buttonholes and silver numbered buttons. Hats laced silver.

46th (Duke of Cornwall's Light Infantry, 2nd Battalion)
(F) Pale Yellow, (L) Square, (O) Silver.
Arrived with Cornwallis, Cape Fear, May 1776. Fought in New York campaign of 1776, Germantown, Monmouth. Flank companies remained in America when the regiment went to Florida then on to West Indies in 1778. Light company men wore red feathers in their caps as a sign of bravado.

47th (The Loyal Regiment (North Lancashire))
(F) White, (L) Square, (O) Silver.
Arrived Boston, October 1774. Fought at Lexington and Bunker Hill. Went to relief of Quebec in 1776. Then served with Burgoyne until Saratoga surrender in 1777. Interned until 1781 then returned to British Isles. Inspection Report of May 1769 states officers had silver numbered buttons, epaulettes and hats with silver scalloped lace.

49th (Royal Berkshire Regiment (Princess Charlotte of Wales'))
(F) Full Green (very dark blue green), (L) Bastion, (O) Gold.
Arrived in Boston, June 1775. Fought in New York campaign of 1776, Brandywine, Germantown. Battalion companies went to Florida, November 1778 then on to West Indies. The light company was under the command of Francis Dundas of the Guards and adopted the red cap feather.

50th (Royal West Kent Regiment (The Queen's Own))
(F) Black, (L) Square 2, (O) Silver.
Arrived in New York, July 1776 in detachments. Men were used to bring up to strength regiments depleted at Bunker Hill. Staff returned to British Isles in August 1776. In 1777 the light company are noted as having shoulder pouches rather than 'belly-boxes'.

52nd (Oxfordshire and Buckinghamshire Light Infantry, 2nd Battalion)
(F) Buff, (L) Square, (O) Silver.
Arrived in Boston, October 1774. Were at Lexington (flank companies) and Bunker Hill where they suffered heavy casualties. Grenadier company had only eight men left unharmed at end of action. Regiment served in New York campaign of 1776–78. Returned to British Isles in August 1778.

53rd (King's Shropshire Light Infantry)
(F) Red, (L) Square, (O) Gold.
Arrived in Quebec, May 1776. Battalion companies in Canada until 1787. Flank companies with Burgoyne until surrendering at Saratoga. Returned home in 1781. Inspection Report of May 1775 states officers had gold embroidered buttonholes, gold numbered buttons, gold laced hats and red and gold sword knots.

54th (Dorset Regiment, 2nd Battalion)
(F) Popinjay Green (dull yellowish green), (L) Square, (O) Silver.
Arrived with Cornwallis, Cape Fear, May 1776. Served in New York campaign 1776, Rhode Island Connecticut. Went to Nova Scotia in 1782.

55th (The Border Regiment, 2nd Battalion)
(F) Dark Green (very dark blue green), (L) Square, (O) Gold.
Arrived Boston, December 1775. Fought in New York campaign of 1776, Brandywine, Germantown. Went to Florida, November 1778 then on to West Indies. Inspection Report of May 1775 states officers' buttonholes looped with narrow gold lace, numbered buttons, gold laced hat, gold epaulettes. Gilt sword with crimson and gold knot.

57th (Middlesex Regiment (Duke of Cambridge's Own))
(F) Bright Yellow, (L) Square, (O) Gold.
Arrived with Cornwallis, Cape Fear, May 1776. Served in New York campaign of 1776. Light company served in Carolina and Virginia down to Yorktown. Went to Nova Scotia in 1783. Light company wore red cap plumes. Inspection Report of May 1775 gives gold epaulettes, numbered buttons and gold laced hats for officers. Gilt swords with red and gold knots.

59th (East Lancashire Regiment, 2nd Battalion)
(F) Purple (pinkish crimson), (L) Square, (O) Gold.
Arrived Massachusetts, August 1774. Flank companies at Lexington and Bunker Hill. Returned to British Isles in December 1775. Facings were ordered to be changed to black from February 1776.

60th Royal American Regiment (King's Royal Rifle Corps)
(F) Blue, (L) Square, (O) Silver.
Small numbers of 1st and 2nd Battalions in America. 3rd and 4th Battalions served in the South. The remainder went to New York in 1782 then on to Nova Scotia in 1783. King's cypher and crown badge on Colours, drums and grenadier caps. Grenadier company is noted as having two fifers besides the drummer. Inspection returns for 1783 give two black pioneers in each company. Probably enlisted in America.

62nd (Wiltshire Regiment (Duke of Edinburgh's))
(F) Yellowish Buff (pale), (L) Square, (O) Gold.
Arrived in Quebec, May 1776. Served in Canada then in Burgoyne's campaign of 1776. Surrendered at Saratoga in 1777. Interned until 1781 then returned to British Isles. Inspection Report of May 1775 states that 'hats were cut too small and coats too short, almost jackets'.

63rd (Manchester Regiment)
(F) Deep Green (very dark), (L) Square, (O) Gold.
Arrived Boston, June 1775. Flank companies at Bunker Hill. Served in New York campaign 1776, then under Cornwallis in Georgia and Carolinas where some mounted companies served as dragoons. When Yorktown surrender came regiment was in action at Eutaw Springs with Lord Rawdon's force. Left Charleston in 1782 with Loyalists for West Indies. Returned to British Isles in 1783. Inspection Report for May 1769 gives for officers, silver embroidered buttonholes and numbered buttons, green epaulettes embroidered silver, silver-laced hats.

64th (North Staffordshire Regiment (The Prince of Wales'))
(F) Black, (L) Square, (O) Gold.
Arrived in Boston 1773. Served in New York campaign of 1776. At siege of Charleston in 1780 and helped garrison the town on its surrender. With Lord Rawdon's force at relief of Fort Ninety-Six and Eutaw Springs. When the Carolinas were abandoned the regiment went to West Indies in 1782.

65th (York and Lancaster Regiment)
(F) White, (L) Square, (O) Silver.
Arrived Boston, October 1774. Flank companies at Bunker Hill. Went to Nova Scotia in May 1776

69th (Welch Regiment, 2nd Battalion)
(F) Willow Green (dark dull green), (L) Square, (O) Gold.
Arrived New York, September 1781, and left for West Indies after only six weeks.

70th (East Surrey Regiment, 2nd Battalion)
(F) Black, (L) Square, (O) Gold.
Arrived Halifax, Nova Scotia, August 1778. Battalion companies served in Canada until 1782. Flank companies served in the South.

71st Frazers Highlanders (disbanded 1783)
(F) White, (L) Square, (O) Silver.
Arrived New York in July 1776. Served in New York campaign of 1776 then with Cornwallis in Carolinas and Virginia. Part of the regiment interned after Yorktown, remainder left Charleston in 1782. Light company wore white waistcoats in place of red. Entire regiment wore 'belly-box'

cartridge pouch. Buttons white metal with number surrounded by wreath. The Light company under Patrick Ferguson (an officer of this regiment) were equipped with the Ferguson rifle.

74th Argyll Highlanders (disbanded 1784)

(F) Yellow, (L) Square, (O) Gold.

Arrived 1778 Nova Scotia, served here and distinguished itself in the defence of Penobscot against an American squadron under Commodore Saltanstat. The flank companies served in the Carolinas.

76th MacDonald's Highlanders (disbanded 1784)

(F) Deep Green, (L) Square, (O) Gold.

Raised in 1777, served in Carolinas and Virginia campaign down to Yorktown where interned. Four hundred Highlanders were 'rough and ready mounted' and used as mounted infantry (bridles and saddles are noted as being scarce).

80th Royal Edinburgh Volunteers (disbanded 1784)

(F) Yellow, (L) Square, (O) Silver.

Raised in 1778. Arrived in New York 1779. Served under Cornwallis in Virginia surrendering at Yorktown. Interned until end of war. Not thought to have worn Highland dress.

82nd Duke of Hamilton's Regiment (disbanded 1784)

(F) Black, (L) Square, (O) Gold.

Raised in the Lowlands. Arrived Nova Scotia, August 1778. Only four companies engaged. Three returned in 1782 after serving in Southern campaign of 1779. Light company was interned after Yorktown.

84th Royal Highland Emigrants (disbanded 1784)

(F) Blue, (L) Square 2, (O) Gold.

Raised in 1775 by Lieutenant-Colonel Allan Maclean. Men were generally Scottish settlers from Nova Scotia and ex-soldiers of the old 42nd, 77th and 78th Highlanders. Consisted of two battalions. 1st Battalion helped defend Quebec against General Arnold's attack then served on the frontier. 2nd Battalion served in Nova Scotia with detachments in Carolinas and Virginia. Some were in Yorktown surrender. Some officers are shown in contemporary pictures with black facings. Regiment was generally clothed as 42nd Highlanders. Sporrans in America were made of racoon skin in place of badger.

105th King's Irish Regiment (disbanded 1783)

Raised in Philadelphia in 1778 as 'Volunteers of Ireland' by Lord Rawdon. Served in the South. Made 105th Regiment of the Line in 1782. Left Charleston in same year. Details of facings and lace not known.

Appendix B: Contemporary Notes on Military Life

THESE notes are taken from a contemporary guide to the furnishing and behaviour of an infantry battalion (Simes 1777).

CLOTHING

Upon the arrival of the clothing the quarter-master, or some other officer appointed for the purpose, is to inspect into them, and if he finds them in every particular article agreeable to the patterns sealed by the board of general officers, all the tailors of the regiment are to be assembled at a place allotted, under the command of one, who is esteemed the best qualified to give the proper directions, and to see the orders duly complied with.

A sentry must be posted on the place they work in, to prevent irregularities and to keep them to their stated hours: the quarter-master is frequently to visit them, in order to punish those who do not submit to the regulations, or behave refractory.

The quarter-master's sergeant is constantly to attend them, except some other part of his duty should command his attendance.

When the regiment is to be new fitted the commanding officer is not to make any alteration therein, without further orders.

The new coats, waistcoats, and breeches are to be dipped in clean fresh water and laid in the sun to dry, then each man to be fitted with coat, waistcoat, and breeches; the bottom of every man's coat to be six inches, except the men of the light infantry, which is to be nine inches from the ground when kneeling upon both knees, and hang of an equal length quite round: the waistcoats for the front rank and rear of grenadiers to have twelve holes and buttons of each side; centre rank and front and rear ranks of the battalion to have eleven holes and buttons; centre rank of the battalion ten.

All waistcoats must cover the soldier well, and to be made full in every part: they are to be cut square at the bottom, and to open back from the lowermost buttonhole to the point: which lower button and hole are to cover the lower part of the waistband of the breeches; the back-seam of the waistcoat to be sewed down as low as the lower part of the waistband of the breeches, and to be strengthened at the bottom of the side seam: the new breeches to be double sewed in all the seams, and made to fit easy, full and well; the escutcheon of the bottom of the side-seam of the coat to be well secured from ripping by a neat loop, and the opening of the back-skirt to be sewed down as low as the bottom of the second loop and secured there from ripping by a neat loop;

the bottom of the lapels to be well stitched; the shoulder-straps to be made high on the shoulder, and sewed down flat one inch, so that the remaining part, when un-buttoned, may fall along the arm; and, when buttoned, to be of a sufficient length to contain the shoulder-belt with ease, and no longer: the skirts of the coats to be sewed together, and a piece of red cloth, near three inches long, and almost two in breadth, with a narrow square lace, put on at the corners, and a button in the centre of the cloth; one of these to be sewed to the point of each skirt.

A foraging cap and stopper to be made up, conformable to pattern ones, out of a part of the old coat, and the remainder to be made into breeches, according to the following directions: each man must be taken measure of, and care taken that the lining of the breeches is of strong new linen of about nine-pence per yard; the breeches to be made full in the seat, to come well over the hips and low under the knee, with a strap for the buckle, and four buttons and button-holes on each side. It is necessary that the non-commissioned officers and private men should be furnished with a pair of white ticken breeches of about two shillings and nine-pence per pair, to be made exactly as the breeches before recited, to wear in the summer time on marches, and if ordered to be stationed in a warm climate, the coolness of them will be very acceptable.

Three shirts; two white stocks (or rollers); one black hair stock; one pair of brass clasps for ditto; three pair of white yarn stockings; two pair of linen socks, dipped in oil, to be worn on a march, under spatterdashes, when necessary; two pair of white linen gaiters, if belonging to the guards; one pair of black long gaiters, with black tops for ditto; one pair of half spatterdashes; one pair of linen drawers; one pair of red skirt breeches; one red cap; one cockade; one knapsack; one haversack; one pair of shoe buckles; one pair of garter-buckles; black leather garters; two pair of shoes; one oil bottle; one brush and picker; one worm; one turn-key; one hammer-cap, and one stopper.

DUTIES

An Officer, when dressed for guard, should have his hair queued, his sash, gorget, and espontoon (except in fusilier corps, where they are to carry fusees), buff-coloured gloves, black linen gaiters, with black buttons and small stiff tops, black garters, and uniform buckles.

Sergeants and Corporals, sent on command, are strictly ordered, on their arrival in town, after the men have received their billets, and refreshed themselves, to see that they pull off their gaiters, and appear, in every respect, as at their quarters.

No Sergeants, Corporals, drummers, fifers, or private soldiers, are to appear in the barrack-yard, or street, without their hair being well platted and tucked under their hats; their shoes well blacked, stockings clean, black garters, black stocks, buckles bright, and clothes in thorough repair.

The pioneers are to have an axe, a saw, and an apron, a cap with a leather crown, and a black bear-skin front.

To keep the regiment perfect, they must have two field-days a week, at least, and the manoeuvres often varied; which will improve and direct the Officers, instead of tiring their patience with repetitions of the manual exercise. The Officers, on such days, should have their hair queued, and appear in regimental frock suits with their sashes, gorgets, and espontoons or fusees. The Non-commissioned Officers and private men must plait and tuck up their hair; be fully accoutred; put on their black linen gaiters, tops, and uniform buckles.

Appendix C: Special Badges

Badges of the Royal Regiments and the Old Corps involved in the American War.

Certain regiments were permitted to wear special badges. These were used on the Colours, drums, rear of the grenadier caps above the grenade badge, and on the Bells of Arms. The following details cover only those regiments serving in the American War.

(a) **3rd Foot (The Buffs)**. In the centre of their Colours their ancient badge of the Dragon; the Rose and Crown in three corners of the Second Colour.

On the grenadiers' caps, the King's crest (front) and the Dragon (rear). The Dragon on the drums and Bells of Arms with the rank of the regiment underneath.

(b) **4th Foot (King's Own Royal Regiment)**. In the centre of their Colours the King's cypher on a red ground within the Garter and Crown over it. In the three corners of the Second Colour their ancient badge of the Lion of England. On the grenadiers' caps, the King's crest (front) and the King's cypher and Crown (rear).

King's cypher painted on the drums and Bells of Arms with the rank of the regiment underneath.

(c) **5th Foot**. In the centre of their Colours, St George killing the Dragon, their ancient badge. In the three corners of their Second Colour the Rose and Crown.

On the grenadiers' caps the King's crest (front) and St George killing the Dragon (rear).

The George and Dragon badge painted on the drums and Bells of Arms with the rank of the regiment underneath.

(d) **6th Foot**. In the centre of their Colours their ancient badge of the Antelope. In the three corners of their Second Colour the Rose and Crown.

On the grenadiers' caps the King's crest (front) and the Antelope (rear).

The Antelope badge painted on the drums and Bells of Arms with the rank of the regiment underneath.

(e) **7th Foot (Royal Fusiliers).** In the centre of their Colours the Rose within the Garter, and the Crown over it. The White Horse in the three corners of the Second Colour.

On the grenadiers' caps the King's crest (front) and the Rose within the Garter and the Crown.

The Rose within the Garter and the Crown painted on the drums and Bells of Arms with the rank of the regiment underneath.

(f) **8th Foot (The King's Regiment).** In the centre of the Colours the White Horse on a red ground within the Garter and Crown over it. In the three corners of the Second Colour the King's cypher and Crown.

On the grenadiers' caps the King's crest (front) and the White Horse (rear).

The White Horse within the Garter painted on the drums and Bells of Arms with the rank of the regiment underneath.

(g) **18th Foot (Royal Irish Regiment).** In the centre of their Colours the Harp in a blue field and the Crown over it. In the three corners of the Second Colour the Lion of Nassau, King William the Third's Arms.

On the grenadiers' caps the King's crest (front) and the Harp and Crown (rear).

The Harp and Crown painted on the drums and Bells of Arms with the rank of the regiment underneath.

(h) **21st Foot (Royal North British Fusiliers).** In the centre of their Colours the Thistle within the circle of St Andrew and Crown over it. In the three corners of the Second Colour the King's cypher on Crown.

On the grenadiers' caps the King's crest (front) and the Thistle (rear).

The Thistle and Crown painted on the drums and Bells of Arms with the rank of the regiment underneath.

(i) **23rd Foot (Royal Welch Fusiliers).** In the centre of their Colours the Three Feathers of the Prince of Wales issuing out of the Prince's coronet. In the three corners of the Second Colour the badges of Edward the Black Prince ie a Rising Sun, a Red Dragon and the Three Feathers in the coronet. Motto 'Ich Dien'.

On the grenadiers' caps the King's crest (front) and the Feathers badge (rear).

The three Feathers badge and motto 'Ich Dien' painted on the drums and the Bells of Arms with the rank of the regiment underneath.

(j) **27th Foot (Inniskilling Regiment).** In the centre of their Colours a Castle with Three Turrets, St George's Colours flying above in a blue field with the name 'Inniskilling' over it. No corner devices in the Second Colour.

On the grenadiers' caps the King's crest (front) and the Castle and Name (rear).

The Castle and Name badge painted on the drums and Bells of Arms with the rank of the regiment underneath.

XLII

(k) **42nd Foot (Royal Highland Regiment).** In the centre of their Colours the King's cypher within the Garter and Crown over it. Under it, St Andrew with the motto 'Nemo me impune lacessit'.

In the three corners of the Second Colour the King's cypher and Crown.

On the grenadiers' caps the King's crest (front) and the St Andrew badge (rear).

The St Andrew badge painted on the drums and Bells of Arms with the rank of the regiment underneath.

LX

(l) **60th Foot (Royal American Regiment).** In the centre of their Colours the King's cypher within the Garter and Crown over it. In the three corners of the Second Colour the King's cypher and Crown. (The Colours of the Second Battalion were distinguished by a flaming ray of gold descending from the corner of the first canton of each Colour towards the centre.)

On the grenadiers' caps the King's crest (front) and the King's cypher and Crown (rear).

The King's cypher and Crown painted on the drums and Bells of Arms with the rank of the regiment underneath.

Bibliography:

BIBLIOGRAPHY

HISTORY OF THE BRITISH ARMY, by Fortescue.

A HISTORY OF THE UNIFORMS OF THE BRITISH ARMY, by C. C. P. Lawson.

HISTORY OF THE DRESS OF THE ROYAL REGIMENT OF ARTILLERY, by MacDonald.

UNIFORMS OF THE AMERICAN REVOLUTION, by Lefferts.

MILITARY COSTUME IN EUROPE – 18th CENTURY, by Reynolds.

DISCIPLINE OF THE LIGHT HORSE, by Hinde.

SERGEANT LAMB OF THE 9th and PROCEED SERGEANT LAMB, by Graves.

STANDARDS AND COLOURS OF THE ARMY, by S. M. Milne.

REGIMENTAL COLOURS IN THE AMERICAN REVOLUTION, by Davies.

JOURNALS OF THE SOCIETY FOR ARMY HISTORICAL RESEARCH.

THE CLOTHING WARRANT OF 1768.

CONTEMPORARY INSPECTION RETURNS, RECORDS, PAINT-INGS AND PRINTS.

REGIMENTAL HISTORIES, JOURNALS AND MUSEUMS.